Windows Troubleshooting Series

Mike Halsey, MVP
Series Editor

Apress®

Windows Registry Troubleshooting

Mike Halsey, MVP
Andrew Bettany, MVP

Apress®

Windows Registry Troubleshooting

ISBN-13 (pbk): 978-1-4842-0993-6

ISBN-13 (electronic): 978-1-4842-0992-9

Managing Director: Welmoed Spahr
Lead Editor: Steve Weiss
Series Editor: Mike Halsey
Technical Reviewer: Sander Berkouwer
Editorial Board: Steve Anglin, Mark Beckner, Gary Cornell, Louise Corrigan, James DeWolf, Jonathan Gennick, Robert Hutchinson, Michelle Lowman, James Markham, Matthew Moodie, Jeffrey Pepper, Douglas Pundick, Ben Renow-Clarke, Gwenan Spearing, Matt Wade, Steve Weiss
Coordinating Editor: Kevin Walter
Copy Editor: James M. Fraleigh
Compositor: SPi Global
Indexer: SPi Global
Artist: SPi Global

Distributed to the book trade worldwide by Springer Science+Business Media New York, 233 Spring Street, 6th Floor, New York, NY 10013. Phone 1-800-SPRINGER, fax (201) 348-4505, e-mail orders-ny@springer-sbm.com, or visit www.springeronline.com. Apress Media, LLC is a California LLC and the sole member (owner) is Springer Science + Business Media Finance Inc (SSBM Finance Inc). SSBM Finance Inc is a **Delaware** corporation.

For information on translations, please e-mail rights@apress.com, or visit www.apress.com.

Apress and friends of ED books may be purchased in bulk for academic, corporate, or promotional use. eBook versions and licenses are also available for most titles. For more information, reference our Special Bulk Sales–eBook Licensing web page at www.apress.com/bulk-sales.

Any source code or other supplementary material referenced by the author in this text is available to readers at www.apress.com. For detailed information about how to locate your book's source code, go to www.apress.com/source-code/.

Contents at a Glance

Contents

About the Authors

Mike Halsey is a Microsoft Most Valuable Professional (MVP) awardee and the author of many troubleshooting books including *Troubleshooting Windows 7: Inside Out, Troubleshoot and Optimize Windows 8: Inside Out,* and *Windows 10 Troubleshooting* from Apress. He is also the author of other Windows Troubleshooting books in this series.

Based in Sheffield, UK, where he lives with his rescue Border Collie, Jed, he gives many talks on Windows subjects from productivity to security, and makes help, how-to, and troubleshooting videos under the banner PC Support.tv. You can follow him on Facebook and Twitter as @PCSupportTV.

Andrew Bettany, a Microsoft Most Valuable Professional (MVP) awardee since 2012 (Windows Expert-IT Pro) and Microsoft Certified Trainer, is technical editor of several titles and co-author for Microsoft Press of *Exam Ref 70-687: Configuring Windows 8 (2013)*, and of Microsoft Official Curriculum courses 20687D, 20688D, and 20689D (2014); and is co-author of multiple books in the Apress Windows Troubleshooting series.

A regular speaker at IT professionals' events and at TechEd conferences in North America and Europe, Andrew also devotes time to co-managing the UK-wide community "Windows User Group". He loves to write, travel and enjoy the countryside and lives on a small-holding close to York in North Yorkshire (UK) with his partner Annette and his son Tommy.

About the Technical Reviewer

Sander Berkouwer (MCITP, MCSE, MCT) is a Dutch IT Professional with over fifteen years of experience with projects in large IT environments. He is a contributing blogger at the DirTeam.com / ActiveDir.org Weblogs (blogs.dirteam.com) and the founder and owner of ServerCore.Net. Since 2009, Microsoft has awarded Sander with the Most Valuable Professional (MVP) award and since 2011 he works part-time as an IT Professionals Evangelist for Microsoft Netherlands.

Introduction

Whatever you do on your Windows PC, from installing software and apps, to using GPS hardware, creating 3D models, or intricate embedded security systems and games, the Registry is at the heart of what you do.

Consequently, it's the one common element that's guaranteed to run through all troubleshooting problems. This makes a good knowledge of what the Registry is, how it works, and how you can work with it, an essential skill for any support technician or IT pro.

That's where this book comes in. There have been other Windows troubleshooting books, but none have gone into as much detail about the Registry as you'll find here.

It's not all dry technical code and complex structures, though. There are also a lot of fun and cool things you can do with the Registry to enhance your productivity and enjoyment of using your PC. In this book we've included over 60 of our favorite hints, tips, and tweaks for Windows Vista, Windows 7, and Windows 8.1.

With a good knowledge of the Registry—and there's no better way to learn than to dive in with some hacks—you'll be in a much better position to quickly diagnose and repair Windows and PC problems as you encounter them.

CHAPTER 1

The Architecture of the Windows Registry

The most relevant simile for the Windows Registry in your PC is the human brain It stores all of the key information and code that allows the different parts of your computer, and its operating system and software, to communicate with one another. This includes details about hardware addresses and communications protocols, software installation and configuration files and, of course, the inner workings of Windows itself.

No matter what version of Windows you are using, you will have not one but many registry files, as Windows splits the registry into several main files, which contain all the information relevant to the overall operation of the computer and its hardware, and other files specific to each individual user and their software, settings, and preferences.

Registry files are databases, often large and complex, that the operating system loads into the PC's memory as the computer starts or the user signs in. Without this readily available store of settings, files, and options, nothing can start or operate on the PC at all.

The Registry is similar to the brain in another way, too. It's able to heal itself, but only to a limited extent. While the human body is full of all the building blocks required to repair and rebuild damaged cells and tissue, the brain, like the spinal cord, mostly lacks this self-repair ability. Should the wrong part of the brain is damaged, it simply would be unable to repair itself In the case of the Registry, should the parts of the databases containing the information required to load the Registry Editor, any third-party repair tools, or the System Recovery Options become corrupt, self-repair will be out of the question.

Fortunately, however, the Registry is unlike the human brain in one significant way: you can rebuild and repair it from the outside, and even reset it to an earlier state or wipe it completely and start from scratch. While the prospect of a surgeon or doctor performing such an operation on your own mind might seem disturbing at the least, this book will guide you through the Windows Registry in depth, and show you how to protect configure, and repair your PC's brain under any circumstances.

1

What Is the Windows Registry?

If, like me, you used Windows 3.1 back in the day, you might remember having to manually open a .ini file in the folder for a program or driver and changing or configuring settings that would enable that program or piece of hardware to work.

Every program and hardware driver had its own .ini file, which was a plain ASCII text document, and each one needed configuring individually for each individual PC. This is because there were always minor differences between PCs, such as different drive letter or serial port assignments, so if you imported a .ini file from one Windows 3.1 PC to another it was unlikely to work.

The Registry was Microsoft's answer to this chaos, and it effectively pulled all these individual .ini files together into a single, manageable database.

The Registry as we know it now was first introduced in Windows 95 and Windows NT, and as a core component of the operating system it hasn't changed much since. The reason for this is compatibility with legacy hardware and software is crucial to business users of PCs, and changing the Registry too much would either break everything, or require a complex virtualization engine, effectively running a PC inside a PC (which would present significant security implications if overall performance wasn't to be affected as well).

Over time the Registry has been made more robust and secure, with features such as User Account Control (UAC) preventing malware from writing itself deep into the folder structure where it might never be found.

Despite its size and the tens or even hundreds of thousands of keys it contains, it's quite a straightforward, simple, and robust system to work with, consisting of a fairly simple structure of folders, keys, and values.

Windows Registry Files

If you are using a *modern* version of Windows—by which I mean Vista, Windows 7, Windows 8 or 8.1, and Windows 10—then the Registry, how it is structured and operates, and how you can edit and work with it will be the same. As a core component of the operating system, it doesn't change very often, though there were slight differences in Windows XP and Windows Server 2003 that, where applicable, we will detail in notes throughout this book.

Windows has several stores for Registry files, one for the settings that are relevant to all users on the PC, such as hardware and general operating system options, and more for each individual user.

The main registry files are located in the %systemroot%\System 32\Config\ folder (see Figure 1-1) and consist of the following:

- SAM (Security Accounts Manager)
- SECURITY
- SOFTWARE

- SYSTEM

- DEFAULT

- USERDIFF (used only for OS upgrades)

Additionally, each user will have their own Registry files:

- %userprofile%\ntuser.dat

- %userprofile%\AppData\Local\Microsoft\Windows\UsrClass.dat

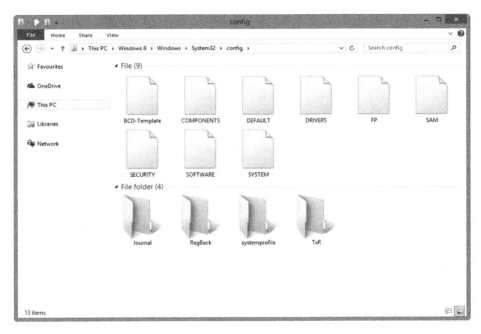

Figure 1-1. *The main Windows Registry files*

The first of these files, ntuser.dat, contains the user's general software, customization, and configuration options. The second, UsrClass.dat, contains additional settings such as user-specific file associations and COM (Component Object Model) information.

■ **Note**   If you are still using Windows XP or Windows Server 2003, please stop! However, the UsrClass.dat file can be found in the %USERPROFILE%\Local Settings\ Application Data\Microsoft\Windows\ folder.

The Registry files themselves are binary format files, and as such are not readable without interpreter software. This is different from .reg files, which are exportable from the Windows Registry Editor and are plain text, so as to be viewable and editable by administrators.

Registry Keys and Values

The Registry, when viewed in its entirety, is split into five main sections, or groups. This helps organize the different keys and folder in the Registry to make them easily navigable.

When you modify or create items in the Registry you will create both keys and values, but what are the differences between the two?

■ **Note**   Registry keys are containers that will contain values for software, hardware or the Windows OS itself. Keys can be thought of as folders, in which the values are individual files. You can navigate the keys using a folder-type hierarchy. Values are the nuts and bolts of the Registry. These are the settings, integers, and strings that provide the data and information that helps Windows load and effectively work with your hardware and apps.

HKEY_CLASSES_ROOT (HKCR)

This section stores information about registered applications, OLE Object Class IDs, and file associations. Sometimes you may see it abbreviated to HKCR.

Should a subkey be added that duplicates a key that already exists in HKEY_CURRENT_USER\Software\Classes, Windows will use the HKEY_CURRENT_USER\Software\Classes key as its master.

HKEY_CURRENT_USER (HKCU)

This section contains the configuration options for the currently signed-in user's profile, including the disk locations for user folders, control panel settings, and specific app configuration settings.

HKEY_LOCAL_MACHINE (HKLM)

As you might expect, this key contains all the settings specific to the PC on which Windows is installed. It contains the subkey files SAM, SECURITY, SYSTEM, and SOFTWARE that I listed earlier. A fifth file, HARDWARE, is created afresh each time the PC starts, and contains information about currently detected plug-and-play hardware.

This key also contains the files COMPONENTS and BCD, which can be found in the %systemroot%\System 32\Config\ folder, and which contain information specific to the PC's boot configuration data.

A few of the subkeys in the HKEY_LOCAL_MACHINE section are worthy of note, because this collection of Registry files is most commonly modified and edited by users.

SAM

The Security Accounts Manager keys section will commonly appear empty unless the viewing user has all appropriate administrative permissions. It contains the security information for all the domains the PC connects to, including the local domain, which is also called SAM.

Each SAM database contains the username used to log in to the domain, along with a UID (Unique Identifier) for the domain, a cryptographic hash of the user's password, the location of the user's Registry Hive, on the server, and various other settings and flags that may be required by the connection.

SECURITY

This subkey also appears empty for most users unless they have appropriate administrative permissions. Upon connection to a domain, it is linked to the security database in the Server Registry Hive, which will contain all security policies applicable to the current user and their installed apps.

SYSTEM

This subkey contains information about Windows setup, settings, and details for currently mounted devices, and for drives that contain a file system.

SOFTWARE

This subkey contains settings for the currently installed Windows installation and its installed software and apps. The keys are organized by software vendor and include subkeys for file extensions, MIME types, and Object Class and Interface IDs (such as ActiveX controls).

HKEY_USERS (HKU)

The HKU key contains settings and options for the currently-loaded user profile. You cannot access settings for any user account other than the currently signed-in user through these keys.

HKEY_CURRENT_CONFIG (HKCC)

Last, the HKCC keys contain information gathered when the PC starts and Windows loads. This information is relevant only to the current powered-session and is discarded when the PC is switched off.

Within each of the Registry sections, the individual keys include many different types, to allow the greatest flexibility for managing settings and options for the Windows OS and your apps and hardware.

HKEY_PERFORMANCE_DATA

This section is invisible when using the Windows Registry Editor. It contains runtime and performance data that is provided by the Windows kernel, drivers, apps, and services. It is discarded when the PC is switched off and is rebuilt at the next boot.

Registry Value Types

When you create a new Registry value, you will be presented with the following options:

- REG_BINARY: This key type stores raw binary data.

- REG_DWORD: A variable-length 32-bit integer.

- DWORDS: Commonly used to define the parameters for settings, device drivers, and software configuration.

- REG_SZ: A fixed-length string value.

- REG_EXPAND_SZ: An expandable-length string value, also used to contain environment variables.

- REG_MULTI_SZ: A multiple string that may contain a list of values, normally separated by commas or a space.

- REG_RESOURCE_LIST: A list of resources in a nested array, used by device drivers.

- REG_RESOURCE_REQUIRMENTS_LIST: An array list of hardware resources, used by device drivers.

- REG_FULL_RESOURCE_DESCRIPTOR: These are nested arrays used to store the resource lists for physical hardware devices.

- REG_LINK: A symbolic link (UNICODE) to another Registry key that specifies both the root key and the path to the target key.

- REG_NONE: Data that does not have a specific type.

- REG_QWORD: A variable-length 64-bit integer.

■ **Note** There are some differences between 32-bit (x86) and 64-bit (x64) Windows Registries. The 64-bit QWORDs are not supported by 32-bit versions of the Windows operating system. Also, the Registry handles 32-bit and 64-bit keys in the same intelligent way that the file system handles multiple versions of the same DLL files, but maintains a compatibility folder that you can find in the HKEY_LOCAL_MACHINE\Software\WOW6432Node section of the Registry.

.reg Files

Earlier in the chapter I made a reference to .reg files, which are different from the Registry in several important ways. First, while they store Registry keys and values, they are intended for backup and transport between different PCs and Windows installations of those values and keys. Also, .reg files are stored in plain ASCII text, unlike the Registry database files, which are stored in binary.

.reg files will be automatically opened (or at least they should be if the file associations are set correctly on a PC) by the Windows Registry Editor when double-clicked. You can also export the entire Registry, or individual Registry keys, to .reg files in the Registry Editor itself; we will show you how to perform these actions in Chapter 2.

You can manually edit the contents of a .reg file in Windows Notepad, or any other text file editor (see Figure 1-2). Right-clicking a .reg file in File Explorer (known as Windows Explorer in Vista and Windows 7) will reveal an Edit option in the context menu that appears.

Figure 1-2. *Editing the contents of a .reg file in Notepad*

In the example seen in Figure 1-2 the key is listed as HKEY_CURRENT_USER\Control Panel\Desktop\WindowMetrics, and I have highlighted it here as it includes an addition to the default configuration.

At the end of the key sits a subkey called `"MinWidth"` that has an integer value of 54. This key changes the behavior of the Never Combine, Hide Labels option for the Windows Taskbar (not Vista) so that program icons appear separately when multiple instances of that program are run, but without their text labels.

We will include many more hints, tips, hacks, and tweaks for the Windows Registry in Chapter 6.

Summary

Overall, while the Windows Registry is a huge behemoth bloated with many thousands of complex binary, hexadecimal, and ASCII values and codes, it's fairly simple and straightforward to work with. In the next chapter, we'll look how you can do exactly that, and what tools and utilities exist to help you.

CHAPTER 2

∎ ∎ ∎

Registry Tools and Utilities

Because of the complexity of a PC system, with its OS components, software, apps, hardware, and drivers, the Registry can swell to a significant size. On my own PC, as I sit and write this, the Registry files are over 225MB combined. If you wanted to open these files in a text editor, such as Windows Notepad, they would take a long time and be very complex indeed.

It's a good thing, then, that the Registry is a binary database, rather than a text file, and that dedicated tools exist to help you open, edit, and work in other ways with the Registry. In this chapter we'll show you around the most common and popular tools and utilities.

RegEdit

The most logical place to start is Windows's built-in Registry Editor, RegEdit (see Figure 2-1). You can find this by searching for `Regedit.exe` in the Start menu or at the Start screen; it will require elevated administrator privileges to run.

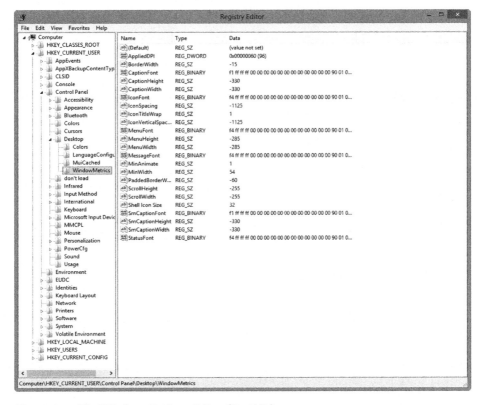

Figure 2-1. *The Windows Registry Editor (RegEdit)*

The built-in Registry Editor is a fairly basic editing and viewing app for the Registry, but then it doesn't have to do much. For the majority of the time all you will need to do with the Registry is back up and reimport Registry files, and view, create, modify, and delete individual keys and values. To summarize, the Registry Editor allows you to perform the following operations:

- Locate a subtree, key, subkey, or value
- Add a subkey or a value
- Change a value
- Delete a subkey or a value
- Rename a subkey or a value

File Menu

There is a standard menu at the top left of the Registry Editor window with File, Edit, View, Favorites, and Help options. The File Menu (see Figure 2-2) contains the Import and Export controls and you can use these to back up and restore individual keys, settings for whole applications or devices, or the entire Registry.

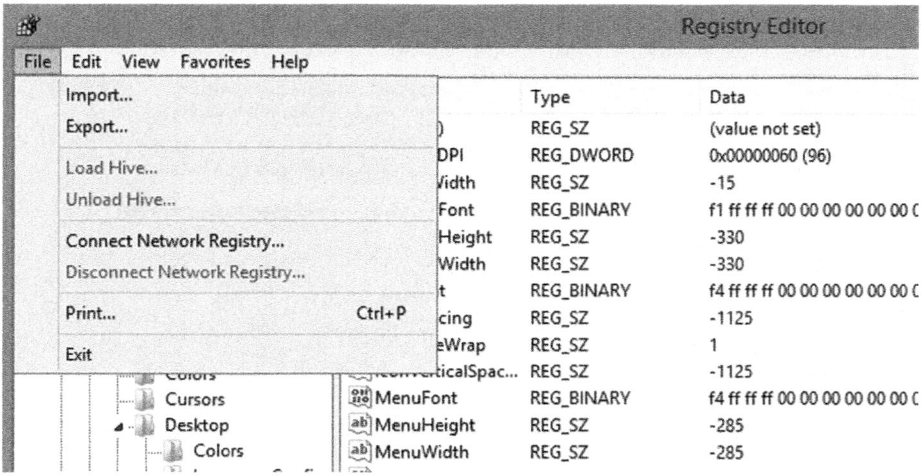

Figure 2-2. *Back up and restore the Registry in the File menu of the Registry Editor*

■ **Note**   Always make a backup copy of the Windows Registry before creating, editing, or modifying any keys or values, in case an action you perform causes an app, a hardware device, or Windows itself to become unstable or unresponsive. You can back up the Registry in the File menu of the Registry Editor by selecting Export. You can also force Windows to make a backup of the Registry by creating a System Restore point, as described in Chapter 3.

Backups of the Registry are saved with the registration file (.reg) extension, which are plain text and can be opened with Notepad, as shown in Figure 2-3. This means that it is always advisable to store your .reg backup files in a secure and encrypted location, as any plain-text file in the workplace that might be susceptible to theft by an individual or through the use of malware might reveal sensitive data, such as domain information, that you would not wish revealed.

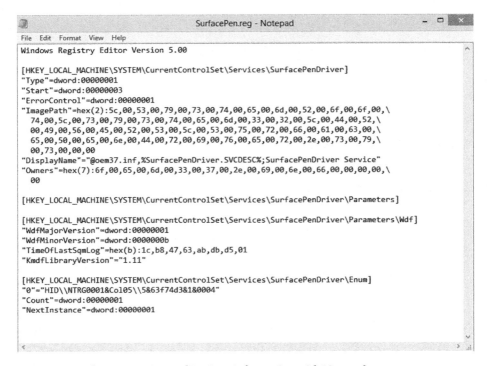

Figure 2-3. *Edit or view exported Registry information with Notepad*

Typically a .reg file will contain Registry information exported from one Registry. If this .reg file is then run on another system, the information contained in the .reg file will be imported directly into the Registry.

■ **Note**   For a user to work with the Registry Editor or import .reg files directly to the Registry, they will require elevated administrator privileges.

Also in the File menu are options to load and unload a Hive. This is a file that contains a portion of the Registry but that may be currently inactive, such as being applicable for a different user on the machine or not being applicable to the current Windows session (e.g., if you've booted from a Windows install disc and are editing the Registry from that).

Load and Unload Hive will permit you to manage these additional Registry files for viewing and editing. By default in Windows these options are grayed out and unavailable until you select HKEY_LOCAL_MACHINE (HKLM) or HKEY_USERS (HKU). We will show you how to edit Registry Hive files, including the files for other users, in Chapter 4.

The next menu option allows you to connect to a Network Registry. If you have a computer with Remote Administration enabled that is running the Remote Registry Service, you can use this function to access Registry files on that PC. Remote administration will be covered in Chapter 4.

Edit Menu

The Edit menu in RegEdit (see Figure 2-4) provides the commands you need to create new Registry keys and to edit and delete existing keys and values. All of this functionality is also available by right-clicking in RegEdit as well.

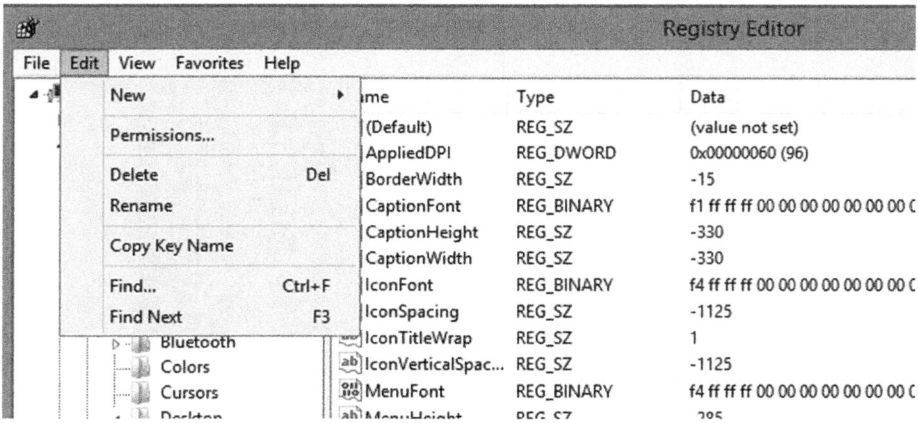

Figure 2-4. *Manage Registry permissions in RegEdit's Edit menu*

Under the Edit menu you can also set access permissions for the Registry. This can be useful if you need to manage the Registry files for other users on the PC, but find that file access is blocked when you do so.

Clicking Permissions in the Edit menu will display a Windows security dialog containing a list of users and administrators on the PC, along with straightforward Allow and Deny check boxes, as shown in Figure 2-5. You can modify access permissions here for the Registry files.

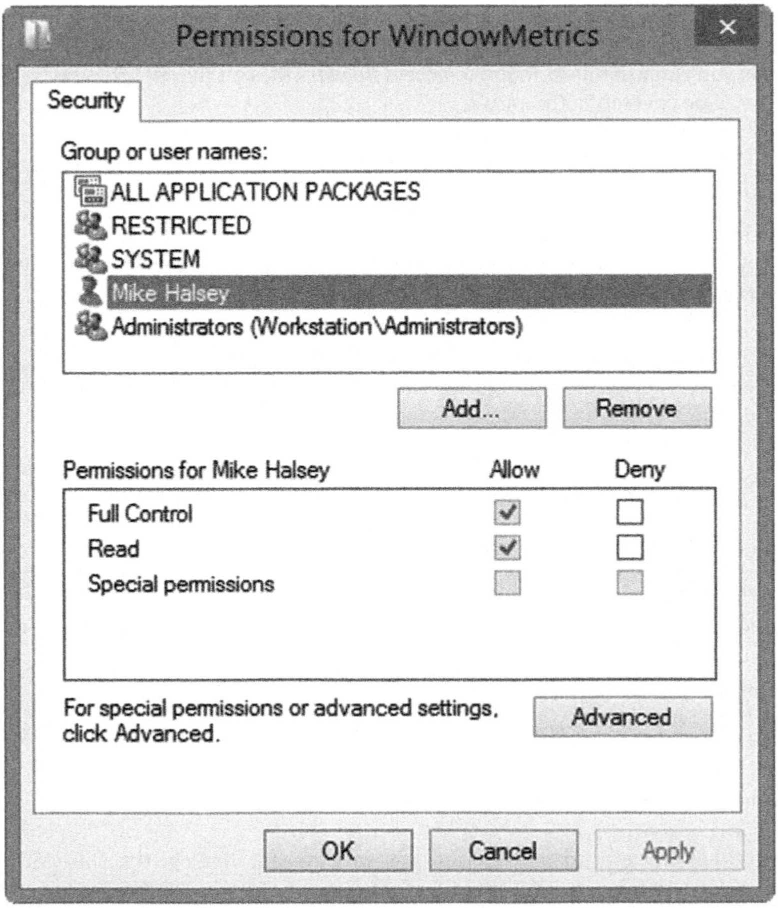

Figure 2-5. *Managing Registry access permissions*

Registry keys can be created by choosing the appropriate option in the Edit menu, or by right-clicking on any Registry key (to edit it) or in a blank space (to create one) as shown in Figure 2-6.

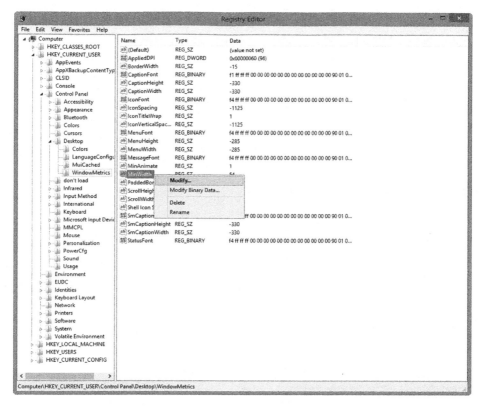

Figure 2-6. *Creating and editing Registry keys*

The main tree view of the Registry in the left panel of RegEdit, as shown in Figure 2-7, also allows you to manage, create, and delete whole key groups. Right-clicking on a group presents the same options as right-clicking on an individual key, with the addition of Export and Permissions options. The Export option can be useful for saving just the keys required for a particular customization, option, app, or hardware device for use on additional PCs.

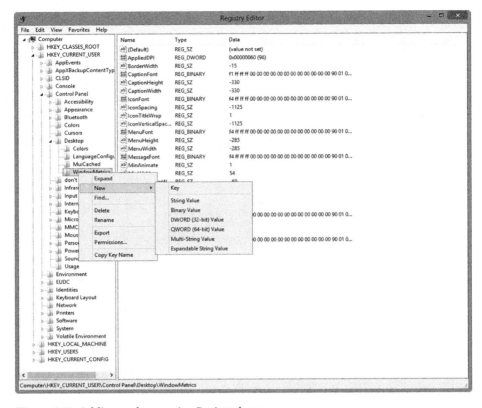

Figure 2-7. *Adding and managing Registry keys*

REG.EXE and REGINI.EXE

You can also modify the Windows Registry directly from the Command Prompt (if you are running the Command Prompt with elevated administrator privileges).

The commands you can use with the Console Registry Tool for Windows (REG.EXE) are *add, compare, copy, delete, export, import, load, query, restore, save* and *unload*. Let's look at the syntax for each of these commands.

■ **Note**   By default, Reg.exe works to match the version of Windows that is installed, be this 32 bit or 64 bit, To work specifically with other key types you can use REG.EXE with the /reg:32 and /reg:64 switches.

Add is used to add keys or subkeys to the Registry and is used in the following format (note that some of the variables and syntax will be uniform across REG.EXE commands and as such will only be detailed once):

```
REG ADD <KeyName> [{/v ValueName | /ve}] [/t DataType] [/s Separator]
[/d Data] [/f]
```

Use *Add* to add keys or subkeys to the Registry, as shown in Table 2-1.

Table 2-1. *Reg.exe command line switches*

<KeyName>	The key or subkey optionally specifying the \\<ComputerName>\, where omitting \\<ComputerName>\ causes the command to default to the local computer.
	Use HKLM, HKCU, HKCR, HKU, and HKCC for the main keys or HKCU\ Software\Microsoft\Windows\CurrentVersion to address subkeys.
/v <ValueName>	The Registry entry to be added to the specified key or subkey: e.g., /v MidWidth
/ve	Used to specify the Registry entry; should have a null value
/t <Type>	Specifies the type for the Registry entry; use REG_SZ, REG_MULTI_SZ, REG_DWORD_BIN_ENDIAN, REG_DWORD, REG_BINARY, REG_DWORD_ LITTLE_ENDIAN, REG_LINK, REG_FULL_RESOURCE_DESCRIPTOR, REG_EXPAND_SZ,
/s <Separator>	If adding a data type such as REG_MULTI_SZ, specifies the character used to separate multiple instances of data; the default is /0
/d <Data>	Specifies the data to add to the Registry key
/f	Forces the Registry change and skips the prompt for confirmation

Use *Compare* to view the similarities and/or differences between two Registry keys, as shown in Table 2-2, using the following format:

```
REG COMPARE <KeyName> <KEYNAME2> [{/v ValueName | /ve}]
[{/oa | /od | /os | /on}] [/s]
```

Table 2-2. *Reg.exe switches to compare Registry keys*

/v	Specifies the value name to compare
/ve	Specifies that only entries with null value names should be compared
/oa	Displays all the differences and matches
/od	Displays only the differences
/os	Displays only the matches
/on	Does not display results
/s	Compares all subkeys and entries in a recursive way

You can make a copy of a Registry key with *Copy*, as shown in Table 2-3, using this format:

```
REG COPY <KeyName> <KeyName2> [/s] [/f]
```

Table 2-3. *The Reg.exe switch to copy subkeys*

/s	Copies all subkeys and entries under the specified key

Use *Delete* to discard a Registry key, as shown in Table 2-4, using the following format:

```
REG DELETE <KeyName> [{/v ValueName | /ve | /va}] [/f]
```

Table 2-4. *The Reg.exe switches to delete keys and entries*

/v	Deletes a specific key; if not specified all entries and subkeys will be deleted
/ve	Only deletes entries with a null value
/va	Deletes all entries under the specified key but *not* subkeys

Use *Export* and *Import* to make and restore backup copies of Registry keys (see Table 2-5):

```
REG EXPORT <KeyName> <FileName> [/y]
REG IMPORT <FileName>
```

Table 2-5. *The Reg.exe switches to overwrite existing files*

<FileName>	The path and name of the .REG file to create
/y	Overwrites any existing file without confirmation

Use *Flags* to check the virtualization status or to set virtualization for a Key (i.e., to maintain application compatibility), as shown here and in Table 2-6:

```
REG FLAGS <KeyName> [QUERY | SET [DONT_VIRTUALIZE:STATUS]
[DONT_SILENT_FAIL:STATUS] [RECURSE_FLAG:STATUS]] [/reg:32 | /reg:64]
```

Table 2-6. *Reg.exe flags*

QUERY	Display the current flags for the key
DON'T_VIRTUALIZE	Set the key to not permit UAC virtualization
DON'T_SILENT_FAIL	Set the Silent Fail flag for the key
RECURSE_FLAG	Sets recursion of flags on all subkeys
:STATUS	Specify :SET or :CLEAR
/reg:32	Specifies the key should be accessed using the 32-bit Registry view
/reg:64	Specifies the key should be accessed using the 64-bit Registry view

Use *Load* to write previously saved subkeys into a different subkey in the Registry. Use *Query* for operations such as troubleshooting Registry entries; it is intended for use with temporary files (see Table 2-7).

```
REG LOAD <KeyName> <FileName>

REG QUERY <KeyName> [{/v ValueName | /ve}] [/s] [/se <Separator>]
[/f <Data>] [{/k | /d}] [/c] [/e] [/t <Type>] [/z]
```

Table 2-7. *Reg.exe search switches*

/f <Data>	Specified the data or pattern that should be queried; use double quotes "" if string will contain spaces
/k	Search in key names only
/d	Search in data only
/c	Makes the query case sensitive
/e	Only return exact matches
/t <Type>	Specifies what specific Registry type to search, REG_SZ, REG_MULTI_SZ, REG_DWORD_BIN_ENDIAN, REG_DWORD, REG_BINARY, REG_DWORD_LITTLE_ENDIAN, REG_LINK, REG_FULL_RESOURCE_DESCRIPTOR, REG_EXPAND_SZ
/z	Includes the numeric equivalent of the Registry type in the search results

Use *Restore* to write previously saved keys and subkeys back into the Registry:

```
REG RESTORE <KeyName> <FileName>
```

Use *Save* to save a copy of specified subkeys to a file:

```
REG SAVE <KeyName> <FileName> [/y]
```

Use *Unload* to remove a section of the Registry previously added using REG_LOAD:

```
REG UNLOAD <KeyName>
```

RegIni is used to modify Registry files using a script contained in one or more text files. The text file will contain REG.EXE commands (see Table 2-8):

```
REGINI [-m <\\ComputerNamee> | -h <HiveFile HiveRoot>] [-I n]
[-o <OutputWidth>] [-b] TextFiles...
```

Table 2-8. *Working with scripts in Reg.exe*

-m <\\ComputerName>	Specifies the remote computer that is to have its Registry modified by the command
-h <HiveFile HiveRoot>	Specifies the local Registry Hive to modify
-i <n>	Specifies the level of indentation to use in the Registry tree structure; default value is 4
-o <OutputWidth>	Specifies the width in characters of the command output to appear in a Command window; default is 240 characters
-b	Forces compatibility with earlier versions of REGINI.EXE when working with different Windows versions
TextFiles	The name of one or more text files containing the scripts

Modifying the Registry Using PowerShell

As an alternative to working with the Registry using RegEdit or the REG.EXE command, you can also use PowerShell, which is built into all modern versions of Windows. PowerShell allows the automation of common tasks such as creating and editing Registry settings in the PC either directly or via Group Policy Objects.

Many more commands for working with and modifying the Registry are available in PowerShell, and each has its own specific syntax. When PowerShell was first released there were just 129 commands; now in Windows 8 there are over 2,000 commands and functions. Indeed, there are no fewer than 57 PowerShell Registry commands, and a full list with their syntax and usage can be found on the Microsoft MSDN website at http://pcs.tv/1x9NW1M.

PowerShell is a vast topic and anything more than a brief introduction is outside of the scope of this book. Since most readers will be administrators working with the Registry, we will assume that you will seek additional knowledge regarding PowerShell if needed.

One of the first issues many beginners find when learning how to use PowerShell is that a command (cmdlet) may not work as expected. A very common issue relates to correctly setting the `Set-ExecutionPolicy`. To enable tests of your PowerShell scripts within your virtual-lab test environment, you will need to open a new PowerShell command console with administrative privileges and type the following within the PowerShell command window:

```
Get-ExecutionPolicy
```

You should see that PowerShell is by default set to restricted—that is, to only allow scripts that are digitally signed to run. You need to change that policy to unrestricted to allow our scripts to work in our lab environment. Type the following:

```
Set-ExecutionPolicy Unrestricted
```

When the cmdlet runs, you will be given a warning. Type Y to accept the policy setting. This command modifies a key within the Registry to allow scripts to run on your PC without requiring that they be signed first. You will see later in this chapter the exact setting within the Registry that this command changed.

PowerShell can modify settings in the Registry, File System, Certificate Store, and other areas, which PowerShell classes as Drives. Within PowerShell, type:

```
Get-PSDrive
```

You will be presented with the current list of drives that PowerShell has the ability to interact with.

Noice that PowerShell has access to two Hives within the Registry: `HKEY_CURRENT_USER` and `HKEY_LOCAL_MACHINE`. Just like the file system, you can navigate within the Registry structure through PowerShell. Try typing the following (don't forget the colon!):

```
CD HKCU:
DIR
```

If you want to view the properties of a Registry key, you can type:

```
Get-ItemProperty -Path HKLM:\SOFTWARE\Microsoft\PowerShell\1\ShellIds\
Microsoft.PowerShell
```

You should see the properties of the key and this should correlate with the setting you configured earlier in this chapter.

If you wanted to set the value back to Remote Signed, you would type:

```
Set-ItemProperty -Path HKLM:\SOFTWARE\Microsoft\PowerShell\1\ShellIds\
Microsoft.PowerShell -Name "ExecutionPolicy" –Value "RemoteSigned"
```

System administrators will also use Group Policy and Group Policy Preferences to configure PCs within an enterprise. There are several PowerShell commands that can be used when working with the Group Policy Preferences that set Registry values as shown in Table 2-9.

Table 2-9. *Setting Registry Values*

Verb	CMDLETS
Get	Get-GPPrefRegistryValue
	Get-GPRegistryValue
Set	Set-GPPrefRegistryValue
	Set-GPRegistryValue

■ **Note**   You cannot use PowerShell to manage Registry settings that affect the security settings or software installation settings on a PC.

ScanReg

If you are using a "legacy" or older PC, rather than a modern operating system, you may still need to manage or repair your Registry. The Windows Registry Checker Tool (Scanreg.exe) was included with Windows 98, ME, and NT. Microsoft provided this tool for users to be able to fix issues, optimize the Registry, and back up or restore the database.

To access the ScanReg tool, restart the PC in a special startup mode called "Safe Mode Command Prompt Only." In Windows 98 a daily backup of the Registry would be created. Restore the most recent Registry as follows:

- Type cd\windows\command at the prompt, then press Enter.
- Type Scanreg.exe/restore.
- Select the required backup of the Registry from the list, then press Enter.

The PC will restore and then you can restart the PC.

A GUI version of the tool ScanRegw is also available, which can be invoked by selecting Run from the Start menu and typing scanregw. The result is shown in Figure 2-8.

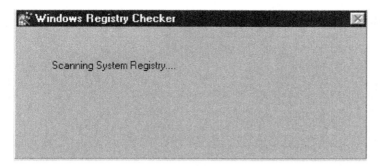

Figure 2-8. *Legacy Registry maintenance with ScanRegw*

■ **Note** ScanReg has been deprecated and is no longer included in modern versions of Windows.

Process Monitor

Process Monitor (ProcMon) is one of the most comprehensive and powerful tools that you should consider using when working with the Registry. Sure, the built-in RegEdit tool can provide you with basic editing and functionality for occasional use, but the abilities of the Process Monitor soon make the default tool very amateurish.

Process Monitor is not included in Windows but is a free tool from Microsoft that has been created by the Sysinternals team and is fully supported by Microsoft. You can either download and install it, or run it directly from the Sysinternals website, at `http://technet.microsoft.com/sysinternals`.

Process Monitor allows you to monitor, record, and save Windows activity in real time (i.e., dynamically). It looks at all file system, Registry, and process/thread activity with the ability to log, analyze, and filter the results (see Figure 2-9). We are primarily interested in its ability to focus on Registry activity. Many forensic and digital investigators consider the tool the de facto advanced monitoring tool for Windows systems due to its advanced features, including live filtering and the ability to save session details in Process Monitor Format (PML), which further allows the data to be loaded into Process Monitor for subsequent analysis.

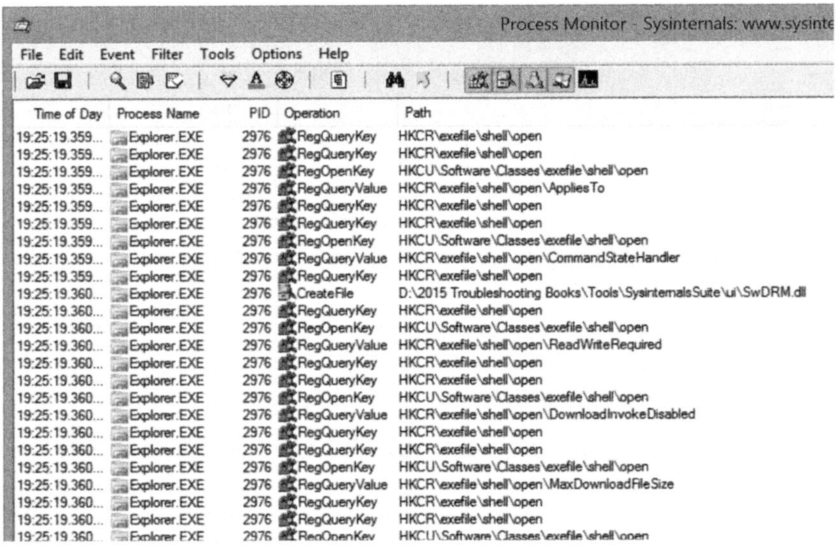

Figure 2-9. *Process Monitor*

■ **Note** The two legacy Sysinternals utilities, FileMon (File Monitor) and RegMon (Registry Monitor), have been combined into the current Process Monitor tool.

You can see in Figure 2-9 that without filters applied, Process Monitor can capture a staggering amount of data—over one million events were recorded within just 10 minutes. It is very important to understand how to apply filters to drill down and focus on the data that you need.

One of the most useful features of the tool is the ability to apply and subsequently save filters for later use. The underlying data is still available regardless of the filters applied—if you remove the filters, then all of the data will be restored.

Simple filtering can be applied by using the event-class filter toggle buttons, which are shown in Figure 2-10 on the toolbar above the activity screen.

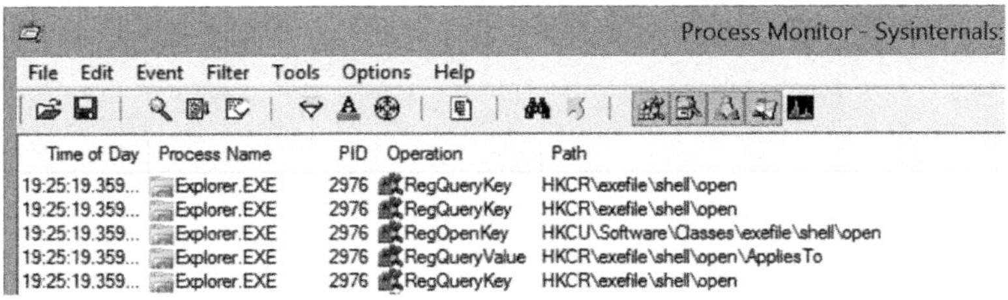

Figure 2-10. *Toggling the built-in event-class filtering buttons*

As shown in the column selection dialog (Figure 2-11), Process Monitor can display a vast array of data, such as the time, date, type, path, username, and whether the process is running in UAC virtualization mode.

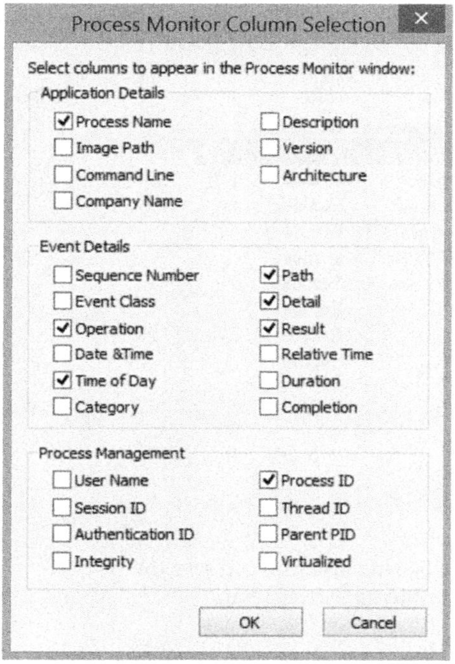

Figure 2-11. *Process Monitor column selection options*

While the built-in filtering may appeal initially, most users will need more advanced filtering. Process Monitor can filter the results on each of the columns and combine results using the Boolean operators OR and AND. To build your own filter, type Ctrl+L or select Filter from the menu bar and then select Filter.... With the Process Monitor Filter dialog box open, use the drop-down menus to select which column heading to filter and whether the item is included or excluded. Wild cards are also allowed within the filtering; for instance, "Operation begins with Reg" will filter activities that affect the Registry, as shown in Figure 2-12.

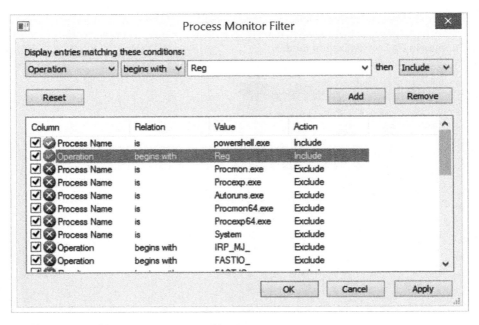

Figure 2-12. *Building Process Monitor filtering*

If you create a set of filters that you would like to reuse, you can save the configuration by using the Save Filter option within the Filter menu.

■ **Note**   Process Monitor will collect data continuously after you open the tool. Each subsequent filter applied will filter through an increasing amount of data. Consider clearing the output by stopping the capture, applying the filter, and then restarting the capture.

Earlier in this chapter you used PowerShell to change the ExecutionPolicy on your computer. To illustrate the power of Process Monitor, we created a filter to capture only the Registry activity by the PowerShell.exe process before the Set-ExecutionPolicy command was run. You can see the results in Figure 2-13. The entry that set the Registry value is highlighted.

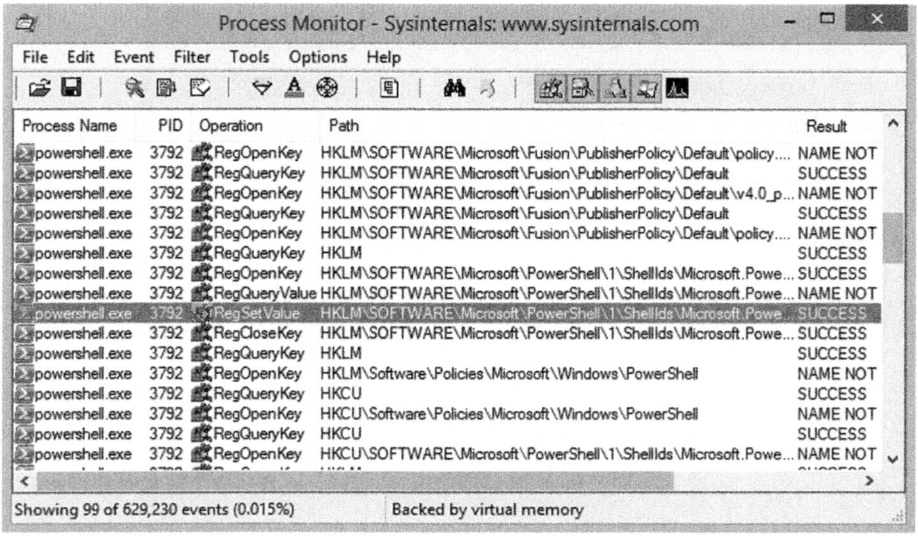

Figure 2-13. *Using Process Monitor to identify changes made to the Registry*

You can right-click the entry in Process Monitor and select Jump to from the context menu to open the Registry and view the newly modified entry. If you just want to see the details of the modification you made, select Properties from the context menu of the item as shown in Figure 2-14, which clearly shows the successful change of status to Unrestricted.

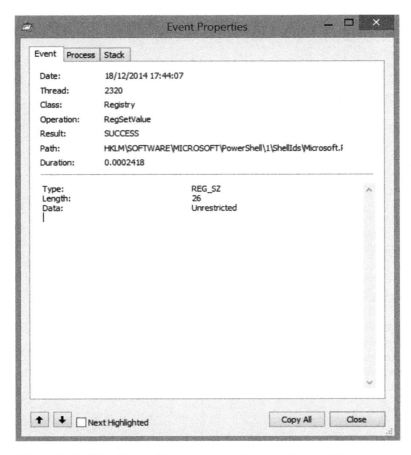

Figure 2-14. *Using Process Monitor to view the properties of a Registry entry*

We will revisit the Process Monitor tool in Chapter 3 to troubleshoot common problems often found within the Registry.

Registry Cleaners

There is some debate about the relative merits or drawbacks of third-party Registry cleaners and utilities and whether, especially on a fast, modern PC, they provide any useful functionality at all. For those people who do like to clean their Registry, however, the most popular tool is the free CCleaner (Figure 2-15), which can be downloaded from www.piriform.com/ccleaner.

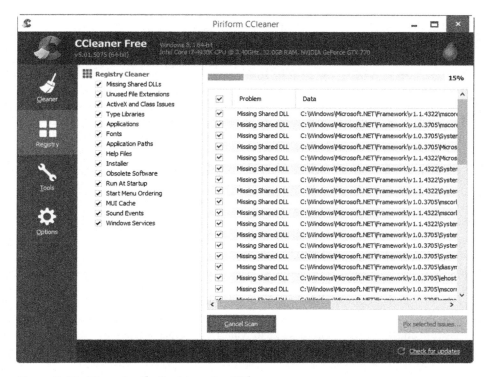

Figure 2-15. *Managing the Registry using CCleaner*

CCleaner is a trusted utility that will automatically prompt you to make a backup copy of your Registry before performing changes to it. It will then search for orphaned (i.e., unused and unlinked) Registry keys and remove them. Using a Registry cleaner can reduce the overall size, and therefore load time, of the Registry databases, and prevent data corruption. Table 2-10 lists a number of popular third-party Registry cleaners.

31

Table 2-10. *Popular Third-Party Registry Cleaners*

Tool	Cost	OS	Download URL
AML Free Registry Cleaner	Free	Windows XP/2003/ Vista/Windows 7/ Windows 8 (32 and 64 bit)	`http://www.amltools.com/`
Auslogics Registry Cleaner	Free	Windows XP/Vista/ Windows 7/Windows 8.1	`http://www.auslogics.com/en/ software/registry-cleaner/ download/`
CCleaner	Free	Windows 8.1, 8, 7, Vista, and XP (32 and 64 bit), but not RT tablet editions	`http://www.techradar.com/ downloads/ccleaner`
EasyCleaner	Free	All versions of Windows: 95/98/ME/NT 3.51 (or newer)/2000/XP	`http://personal.inet.fi/ business/toniarts/ecleane.htm`
JetClean	Free	Windows XP/2000/ Vista/Windows 7/ Windows 8 (32 and 64 bit)	`http://www.bluesprig.com/ jetclean.html`
Offline NT Password and Registry Editor	Free	Supports all Windows from NT3.5 to Win8.1, plus Server versions	`http://pogostick.net/ ~pnh/ntpasswd/`
RegCleaner	Free	Windows XP, 2000, ME, 98, 95, NT	`http://www.techradar.com/ downloads/regcleaner`
Wise Registry Cleaner	Free	Windows XP/Vista/ Windows 7/Windows 8.1	`http://www.wisecleaner.com/ wiseregistrycleanerfree.html`

Summary

While RegEdit is the most well known and perhaps widely used utility for editing and working with the Windows Registry, it's by no means the only one available nor the most flexible—that prize clearly goes to PowerShell.

However you want to work and whatever you're most comfortable with, there's a tool or utility to help you get the job done. Armed with that arsenal, troubleshooting problems in the Registry becomes a simpler task, and it's this troubleshooting that we'll look at in the next chapter.

■ ■ ■

CHAPTER 3

Troubleshooting a Corrupted Registry

From our short exploration of Process Monitor, you can appreciate that for every piece of software that is installed or run on and even removed from a PC, the system will write, query, or delete entries in the Windows Registry. It is therefore vital that you maintain the Registry carefully and ensure that it is kept in good working order.

It is not only that Windows depends on the Registry; applications also store settings and query Registry keys on a regular basis to guide their operational behavior. When corruption occurs, both system and application failures can often be traced to a rogue or incorrect Registry item that can result in error messages and sometimes cause a system to crash.

The main causes of Registry corruption on PCs are...

- Windows Registry corruption

- Software installation or application failure

- Hardware or device driver failure

Windows Registry Corruption

The Registry is a complex database that on occasion can become corrupted. This is, however, quite rare, due to the approach that Microsoft has adopted and refined over the last 30 years of developing Windows. Let us explain.

The Registry is implemented and managed by an executive subsystem called the Configuration Manager (CM). The Registry is made up of several independent Hives, which are then brought together for viewing by the Registry Editor. The CM organizes the Hives on disk and ensures that whenever an application or operating system component reads or changes Registry values or keys, the Registry is always in a recoverable state—even if the PC suffers a crash during Registry modification.

This is achieved by caching parts of the Registry, which allows for very fast search, write, and commit operations. The Registry has evolved from being stored in a simple, flat file structure to benefitting from advances in database technology, so that each in-memory operation is now treated as a transaction and recorded in a special dual-logging scheme. This approach ensures that the transaction will be rolled back if the task could not be completed due to a system failure. Only completed transactions are committed to the Registry.

In addition to the micro-level transactional processing, modern versions of Windows offer self-healing capabilities with features and services such as improvements to New Technology File System (NTFS) and automatic disk check and repair tools, so the underlying file system on which the Registry files are stored remains safe from corruption, thus maintaining Registry integrity.

When a PC is booted, at the beginning of the system boot process, prior to the kernel being loaded (and before the user is presented with the login screen) the Windows Boot Loader also runs some code to ensure the Registry is in a reliable state. If there are inconsistencies, the Boot Loader can perform automatic repairs to fix them before proceeding to load the kernel.

If the system encounters an issue where it needs to invoke a self-heal process, the user will see a pop-up dialog box stating that there was a system error and that the error is being repaired. Once this is completed the PC will continue to load normally.

Software Installation or Application Failure

We have already discussed that during its installation and subsequent configuration, application software writes new Registry keys and updates others with the necessary data to allow the software to work and for Windows to interoperate with the application.

When you use a tool such as Process Monitor, you can witness many hundreds of thousands of key entries and configuration changes to the Registry during a typical installation. Even if you deduct from this number an estimate of the Registry changes that occur normally, you will still see many thousands of Registry interactions. Despite advances in how Registry keys are created, modified, and deleted so that no transaction can be left "orphaned" (i.e., partially complete), this is not the case on older operating systems, on which the "blue screen of death" was often caused by the system not being able to read the expected Registry key due to a write error or power outage corrupting part of the Registry.

On all versions of Windows, the Registry is very susceptible to rogue keys being written during software installations; very often numerous keys are simply left in place even after the software has been uninstalled. Much of the time this is due to an element of laziness by the software author and that during processing, the Registry does not check the robustness of the transactions the software installer has provided.

Software vendors often use the Registry to store and maintain licensing information for the software, which is often locked to the specific user account. In some cases the practice of leaving behind licensing status information in the Registry can be a valid strategy—for example, most trial versions of software will not allow the user to uninstall and reinstall the same software on the same PC in order to gain an additional trial period.

You will also see in Chapter 5 how the prevalence of malware infecting a PC during software installations is entirely preventable, though this is very much dependent upon the usage of the PC, the user account credentials, and whether UAC is in operation.

In summary, over any period of time, whether this is one year or several years, the Registry on your PC will often accumulate a great deal of unwanted, often obsolete information. Unless malware causes other, more serious problems first, the combined effect of this excess clutter will be a bloated Registry, which can lead to degradation of system performance, increased frequency of application errors, and more system freezes and crashes.

Hardware or Device Driver Failure

Hardware and drivers are typically supplied by the hardware vendor and issued as a CD, DVD, or download for the user to install when configuring the device.

For most of the lifetime of Windows, Microsoft has implemented a program that allowed Original Equipment Manufacturers (OEMs), upon payment of a fee, to supply their drivers to the Microsoft Windows Hardware Quality Lab (WHQL) team. The WHQL would extensively test and verify the compatibility of the driver against the selected operating system, and if the driver was functional then Microsoft would digitally sign the driver, include it in its Upgrade Advisor tool (which replaced the Hardware Compatibility List [HCL] used in the XP timeframe), and make it available as part of Windows Update. Hardware vendors could also enroll in Microsoft's "Compatible with Windows XP" or "Certified for Windows 7" programs, or later, the Windows Hardware Certification Program—all of which boosted sales through the reassurance that the device/software would be compatible.

Over the last five years, especially since Windows 7, hardware drivers have become much more robust than those found in Windows XP and especially the troublesome Vista. Windows XP suffered mainly due to the patchwork nature of its own evolution—remember that XP was launched in 2001, years before innovations such as Bluetooth and USB 2.0 had taken hold, and XP did not even Release to Manufacturing (RTM) with a firewall in place. Over its lifespan Windows XP had three major service packs (SPs) as well as thousands of smaller updates during the period that Microsoft still supported it. While this may or may not have created an unstable platform on which OEMs had to write drivers, it did create a headache for the HCL, and OEMs decided not to keep subscribing over and over again to get drivers validated for each SP.

Over time as XP became widely adopted, OEMs cut back on the driver approval process to save money. Without the habit or requirement to produce drivers that would be verified against Microsoft's strict compatibly testing, this resulted in some drivers being released that were incompatible and in several cases very suspect in terms of performance and reliability.

Windows Vista suffered from a number of driver-related issues at the time of release. After a long period of Windows stagnation (remember, Windows XP was very successful and users were reluctant to change), Vista arrived without much OEM support. The lack of adequate driver support was primarily due to Microsoft having changed the way in which Windows worked—Vista was a complete rework as far as the kernel, driver support, and security model. Nearly every legacy driver thus would no longer work with Vista. These legacy drivers would require a complete rewrite—something for which the OEMs did not have the capacity (or, for a period of time, the skilled developers with the up-to-date .NET skills to write them). Writing drivers for the new Windows therefore took some time, both to learn the new skills needed and also to achieve the required driver availability for the installed device population.

■ **Note**   Just as with software installation, it is best practice to reboot the PC after each installation of hardware. This effectively creates a point that is either stable or unstable. Some issues may not present themselves to the user until after a reboot. Both are valuable checkpoints if troubleshooting needs to take place subsequent to the installation.

Resolving Registry Corruption

As we have mentioned, in some cases when the Registry detects inconsistencies in the Registry because "dirty" data has been written, it will attempt to self-repair during the boot-up process. However, while poorly written software and drivers may not pollute the Registry with actual dirty data, they may leave the Registry in an unstable status or with areas of untidiness, which may create system instabilities whenever these areas are accessed.

Windows provides several tools that administrators can use to restore the Registry to a reliable state, including System File Checker, ChkDsk, System Restore, and Driver Rollback. You can also use third-party tools that will help repair, clean, or defragment the Registry.

System File Checker

System File Checker (SFC) is a legacy tool that still works on modern operating systems using an administrative command prompt. SCF seeks to check the integrity of each system file that exists within the Windows installation including Internet Explorer. A corrupted Windows system file can cause system instability and security vulnerabilities, and can lead to suboptimal performance during normal operations.

To invoke SFC, perform the following actions:

- Insert your Windows DVD install media (but do not launch setup).

- Open an administrative command prompt.

- Type: sfc /scannow and press Enter as shown in Figure 3-1.

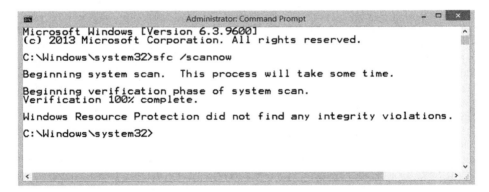

Figure 3-1. *Running System File Checker from the command prompt*

SFC is included with all versions of Windows, but if you are attempting to run SFC on a Windows system that has been updated with one or more service packs, you will need to provide a DVD (or mounted ISO) of the Windows installation files that include the applied service patch. This is because SFC will check and use the SP versions of the system files to replace corrupted files.

■ **Note** SFC will take a long time to complete (the screen capture in Figure 3-1 took one hour). SFC will check each system file for integrity and will repair any damaged system file that it finds.

SFC is not intended to be a regularly used troubleshooting tool; consider using it only when you encounter issues that relate to an unstable system.

ChkDsk

Another legacy tool, Check Disk (ChkDsk and ChkNTFS), will scan the computer's hard drives for errors and fix them. The tool requires administrative credentials to run since it operates at a low hardware level and needs to have exclusive access to the disk if fixing issues.

To run ChkDsk, open an administrative command prompt, type the following, and press Enter, as shown in Figure 3-2.

```
ChkDsk C: /F
```

Figure 3-2. Running ChkDsk from the administrative command prompt

Running the ChkDsk tool on the System drive will result in the task being scheduled to run at the next system restart.

Any hard drive that is starting to fail to read or write data to the disk correctly is very likely to lead to file corruption on the system. Normally if the PC encounters a corrupted data file, this will result in some data loss and ultimately require the user to recover their files from a backup or File History. You should be specifically interested in corrupted Registry files as these can cause the system to hang or, more likely, crash.

Whenever Windows attempts and fails to read data from a corrupted system file, page file, or the Registry, Windows will display a Stop error, commonly known as a blue screen of death. If this happens, you should immediately troubleshoot your system to establish whether this is an isolated incident or whether the blue screen is an early indication of likely drive failure resulting in widespread file corruption and Windows instability. Drive failure may sound catastrophic, and it is, but normally some time prior to this a drive will exhibit the aforementioned failures, which are typical symptoms of bad sectors—areas of a disk that have become unusable. Most bad sectors are caused by physical disturbances such as voltage surges, physical damage, or manufacturing defects.

Software tools such as ScanDisk and ChkDsk are available for users to try to recover data. Typically once a bad sector is identified, the system marks it as bad so it will be hidden from the operating system and never be used again for data.

Windows 8.1 updated the Chkdsk tool so that it will run automatically in the background and actively monitor the health of NTFS volumes. Should a file system corruption be detected, NTFS now self-heals most issues when Windows is running, without requiring the tool to be run from an offline repair tool such as a recovery drive.

■ **Note**   Under normal operational conditions you will not need to run Chkdsk if you use Windows 8.1 as the OS now monitors the file system for corrupted or bad sectors and fixes the problems as a background task.

CCleaner

Although we have already introduced the popular CCleaner tool from Piriform, it is worth including it again here in relation to resolving common Registry corruption issues.

As discussed earlier, whenever software applications and hardware drivers are installed or removed from a PC there will be inevitable issues with leftover or orphaned fragments and incomplete or obsolete entries.

A Registry cleaner will carry out some or all of the following activities:

- Scan your Registry for unwanted/malicious entries

- Remove unwanted/malicious entries to mitigate against Registry bloat

- Remove outdated or superseded files

- Create backups of the Registry

- Remove incorrect file and program associations

- Restore the Registry if any maintenance task fails

- Defragment the Registry to remove any vacant spaces (empty placeholders left behind in the Registry)

- Repair or remove system files such as orphaned or shared DLL files, and locate device drivers no longer required and old ActiveX files

- Schedule scans to ensure that the Registry is scanned and errors are repaired automatically

Many third-party Registry cleaners will remove excess bloat and keys that are no longer relevant to the current system by deleting the unwanted keys and then defragmenting the Registry files.

System Restore

Turned on by default, System Restore has been a key recovery component of Windows for many years and can be extremely useful to recover a system that has encountered a variety of problems. One of the key aspects that we like is that the tool can be used by users of any ability, and can be initiated from either the Graphical User Interface (GUI) or, if the GUI is not stable or accessible, then from the Advanced Startup options within Windows 8.

System Restore is designed to apply a previously working snapshot (or system state) to your PC from an earlier date (such as yesterday or this morning), before it became corrupted, infected, or otherwise problematic—such as an infection with malware or a faulty driver. System Restore can be accessed via System Properties; select System Protection as shown in Figure 3-3.

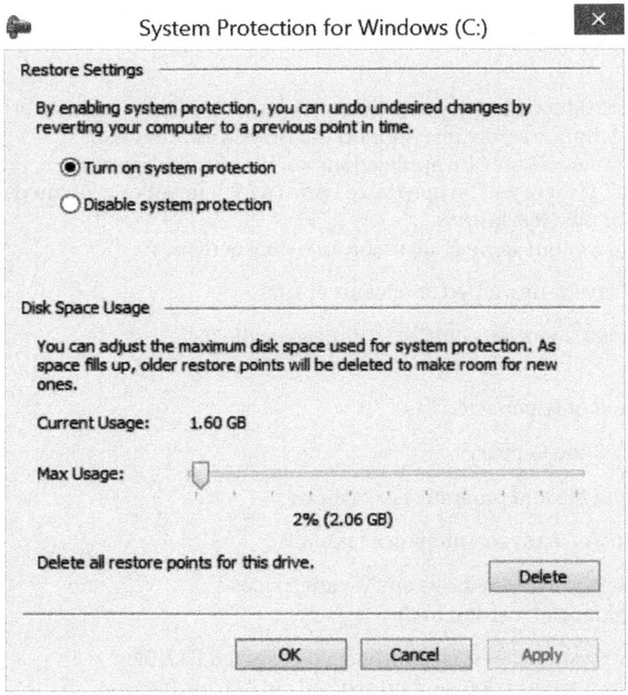

Figure 3-3. *System Restore settings*

■ **Note**   Performing a System Restore does not delete any of your personal files or settings, but you will lose any apps or installed programs that you have added to your system after the date of the chosen System Restore point. The installation files may still be on your PC, but their Registry entries will have been removed.

Windows 7 improved System Restore by allowing users to view a list of applications that might be affected by using System Restore. For any application other than a simple self-contained executable (such as Procmon.exe), this can be a big deal. Newly installed programs will not work after a System Restore recovery because the application entries within the Registry will not be restored during the restoration process, causing the software to fail when launched unless they are reinstalled.

Restore points are stored on the local system and managed by Windows automatically. They will be triggered when the following activities take place:

- Installation of new application

- Installation of device driver

- User manually creates a restore point within the System Properties dialog box by clicking Create... (see Figure 3-4)

Figure 3-4. *System Restore protection settings*

To restore a PC that has become unresponsive or keeps crashing, use one of the following options.

Launch System Restore from Within the GUI

If you are using Vista, Windows 7, or Windows 8, you can launch the System Restore wizard by performing the following steps:

- Select System from the Administrative menu (Windows+X in Windows 8 and 8.1).

- Select System Protection.

- Click the System Restore... button.

- Choose the recommended restore point, or show more restore points (see Figure 3-5).

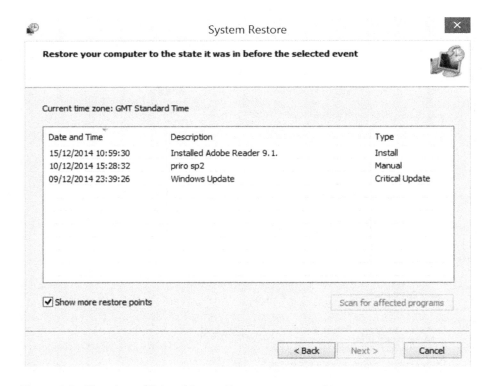

Figure 3-5. *Choosing additional System Restore recovery points*

- Click Next and follow the wizard instructions, allowing the PC to reboot.

- Once the process is complete, Windows will display the System Restore notification screen, which will advise if the process was successful or if the restore point could not be applied.

■ **Note** System Restore has always received mixed reviews from IT professionals; some like the tool, while others have little faith in its abilities. Our experience is that the tool is very credible and works well, especially on well-maintained systems. It remains a valuable tool in our troubleshooting toolkit and, being wizard driven, is generally not prone to user error.

Launch System Restore from the Advanced Options Menu at Startup

On a Windows 7 PC, reboot the system and press F8 during the boot-up phase of startup, prior the "Starting Windows" logo being displayed. You should then see the Advanced Boot Options as shown in Figure 3-6. To start the System Restore wizard, select the Repair Your Computer option.

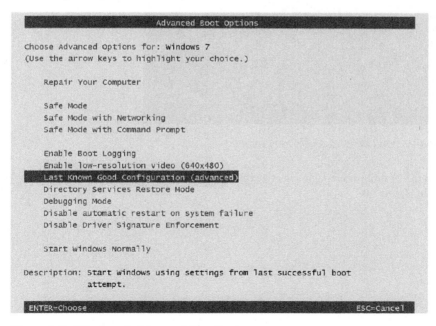

Figure 3-6. Windows 7: Advanced Boot Options

If you are using Windows 8 or later, you can also invoke the Advanced Startup tools from within the GUI. If your PC will not boot into Windows due to startup failure, then the OS should automatically restart in the Recovery Environment and offer you options to help troubleshoot your PC.

If your PC does not offer you the recovery environment, insert your Windows 8 or later DVD or Recovery Disc and follow the "Press any key to boot to the DVD" prompt. Click Next, and then click Repair your computer. On the Choose an Option page, as shown in Figure 3-7, select Troubleshoot. (External link: Windows Recovery Environment (Windows RE) Overview, http://technet.microsoft.com/en-us/library/hh825173.aspx.)

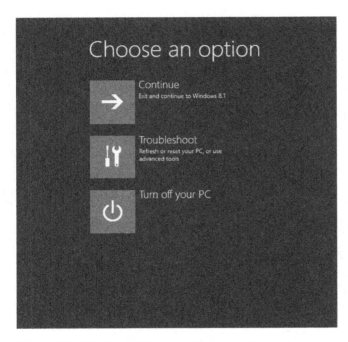

Figure 3-7. *Windows 8: Recovery Environment*

On the Troubleshoot page, select Advanced options, then select System Restore as shown in Figure 3-8.

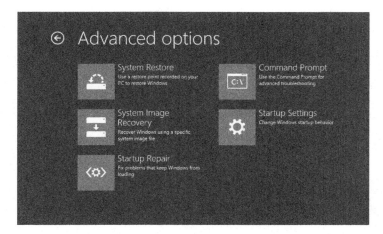

Figure 3-8. *Windows 8: Recovery Environment—advanced options*

On the System Restore screen, choose the operating system that you want to restore and then click Next. The System Restore wizard will now run, and you will be able to follow the wizard as it prompts you to select the appropriate restore point and then restart the PC.

Automatic Startup Repair

Windows 7 and later OSes can now attempt to automatically detect and repair many common startup problems without the need for user intervention. In nearly all scenarios where a PC has difficulty booting or starting, you should allow Windows to troubleshoot and fix the problem before moving on with your recovery plan to a more advanced stage.

In Windows 8 the OS should initiate startup repair if any of the following issues are present:

- Windows fails to startup properly twice

- Windows is restarted unexpectedly twice within two minutes after the startup

- An error is detected during Secure Boot

- A BitLocker-related error is detected during startup on a touch-only device

If you have moved to Windows 8 from an earlier OS such as Windows XP, Vista, or Windows 7 and have tried to invoke the Advanced Boot Options by pressing F8, you will have noticed that this option is no longer available.

To allow a user to see the Advanced Boot Options, you will need to run the following command:

```
BCDEdit /set {bootmgr} displaybootmenu yes
```

You can then reboot the system and enter the Recovery Environment as shown previously, or wait for the command-line option, which allows you to press F8 and boot into the Startup Settings without requiring you to use the Windows DVD, and offers the tools shown in Figure 3-9. Notice that you can use either the number keys or function keys F1 to F9 to select an option.

Figure 3-9. *Windows 8: Advanced Startup Settings*

■ **Note**   By default the system will allow 30 seconds to decide if users wish to enter the boot recovery options during startup. This setting can be set to a lower number (such as 10) by changing the setting within the Startup and Recovery setting dialog box found in System Properties.

Last Known Good Configuration

Although this feature has been part of Windows for many years, most users either have not seen the feature or perhaps have misunderstood it.

If the user is unable to sign in to the system for whatever reason, Windows provides a little-known startup option called "Last Known Good Configuration" as shown in Figure 3-10, which will replace the current system Registry configuration (HKLM\SYSTEM\CurrentControlSet) with a saved version of the Registry in which the boot process had been successful.

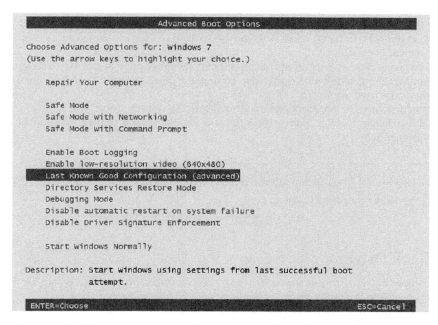

Figure 3-10. *Windows 7: Selecting the Last Known Good Configuration option*

A successful boot relates to the success criteria of each of the following actions:

- Startup of auto-start services
- Load of device drivers
- User account sign in

Last Known Good Configuration should only use this feature if the problem relates to the current signed-in session and the user reported no incidents in the previous login.

The Registry stores information within the HKEY_LOCAL_MACHINE\SYSTEM Hive to indicate whether the system successfully started at the last startup. This information is located in the following subkeys:

- \CurrentControlSet (which acts as a pointer to the ControlSetxxx subkey, where xxx represents a number, such as 001, shown below in the Current value)

- \Select (which contains the following entries: Default, Current, Failed, and LastKnownGood)

During normal Windows startup, the Windows Boot Loader uses the control set given in the \Select\Default value, and if no errors are encountered then the values for the subkeys Default, Current, and LastKnownGood will all contain the same ControlSet subkey, such as ControlSet001.

If the startup process encounters issues and the user fails to sign in to a user account, the subkey for the Failed entry is updated to point to the failed configuration definition so that this is not used again.

In practice most troubleshooting issues relating to the startup process are attributable to corrupt, faulty, or incorrect drivers or loading service configurations and their interdependencies.

■ **Note**   Last Known Good Configuration has been deprecated in Windows 8 and later in favor of the new Recovery Environment.

Roll Back Driver

If an incompatible or corrupted device driver has been installed on the PC, it is very likely to be responsible for any stability issues that may arise following the installation.

If you can sign in to Windows, you should be able to use a feature called Roll Back Driver, which will allow you to replace the updated driver with the previously installed driver, effectively rolling back the driver. In most cases this will resolve the problem. Roll Back Driver is an option found on the Properties tab of the device within Device Manager (see Figure 3-11), and was first introduced with Windows XP.

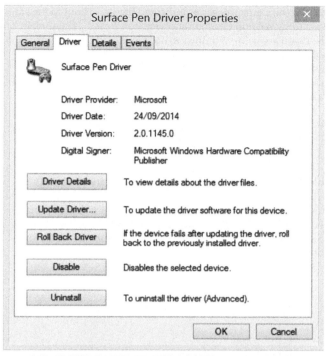

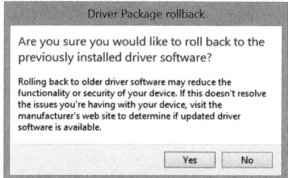

Figure 3-11. *Roll Back Driver feature and confirmation screen in Device Manager*

If the system is very unstable and will not allow normal booting into Windows, you can boot using Safe Mode, which is a version of Windows that loads a minimal set of essential drivers. Once in Safe Mode you should be able to either roll back the driver, or delete it and reinstall a working driver and then reboot.

To boot into Safe Mode, use the same process as indicated before to boot to the same menu that we saw for the Last Known Good Configuration (in Windows 7), then select to boot the PC in Safe Mode. If you are using Windows 8, boot to the Advanced Startup Settings shown in Figure 3-8 and select Enable Safe Mode.

Many of these driver issues have been mitigated over recent years for a number of reasons, including a stable and consistent kernel model introduced with Windows Vista, and also the increased shift toward 64-bit computing, which requires all drivers to be digitally signed.

Summary

However you need to troubleshoot problems with the Registry, there are tools and utilities that help you do it. Even if you're unable to boot to the Windows desktop, you can still use utilities built into the OS to repair problems.

The methods we've detailed so far, though, are primarily aimed at troubleshooting and repairing problems for a single-user PC. If more than one user is set up on the system, things can get slightly more complicated, and this is what we'll deal with in the next chapter.

CHAPTER 4

■ ■ ■

Working with Other Users' Registry Files/Advanced Troubleshooting

Working on the Windows Registry shouldn't ever be an overly difficult or arduous task, especially if it's your own Registry, you need to make changes or troubleshoot a problem for the currently signed-in user, or you need to fix a hardware or general Windows issue. Sometimes, however, you might find that more than one person uses the same PC and you need to make changes to all of their accounts. You can't rely on those other people being around and coming to sign in to the PC when you need them to so you can expedite your repair work.

It is possible, though, to work on the Registry files of more than one user account on a PC from within a single administrator-level account, which can save valuable time, frustration, and the need to save text and configuration files containing all the necessary changes, let alone transport those files from one account to another.

Working on Other Users' Registry Files

We have seen how important the Registry is in relation to Windows and how modifications to the Registry can affect how the PC will operate. Within an enterprise, administrators will often use Group Policy to configure, deploy, and manage applications, settings, and user preferences on PCs within the organization.

We will now discuss how to manage Registry settings on other users' PCs using the following tools:

- Regedit.exe
- Remote Registry Service
- Windows PowerShell
- Group Policy Preferences

RegEdit.exe

RegEdit was introduced in Chapter 2, so we will dive straight into how to use this built-in Windows tool to connect to another Registry on a different PC.

If you are testing this scenario locally, you can export a copy of your own Registry, which you can then import to work with. Open Command Prompt (Admin) either by searching for it in the Start Menu or at the Start Screen, or by pressing Windows+X in Windows 8 or 8.1, and then type the following:

```
C:\mkdir c:\Temp
Regedit.exe /e c:\temp\yourname.reg
```

To load another Registry Hive into the current Hive, follow the steps below:

1. Log on to your computer as an administrator.

2. Type RegEdit at the Start Screen and press Enter.

3. Accept the User Account Control (UAC) warning.

4. Select the HKEY_LOCAL_MACHINE branch.

5. From the File menu, select Load Hive.

6. Locate the Registry file that you want to load and click OK.

7. Provide a friendly name for the loaded Registry file.

Once you have inspected or amended the Registry settings, you should unload the Registry file by selecting Unload Hive from the File menu.

If you want to connect to the Registry owned by another user account, you can run RegEdit.exe as before, but then open the NTuser.dat from the user profile that you wish to access. The NTuser.dat (or NTuser.man for a mandatory user profile) files are found within the Documents and Settings folder for Windows Vista or the Users folder in Windows 7 or later. Essentially you will load another users' Registry Hive file onto your own PC and view them within the HKEY_USERS Hive, as shown in Figure 4-1.

1. Log on to your computer as an administrator.

2. Type RegEdit at the Start Screen and press Enter.

3. Accept the UAC warning.

4. Select the HKEY_USERS branch.

5. From the File menu, select Load Hive.

6. Browse to the profile directory and select NTuser.dat.

7. When prompted for Key Name, input their username as a reference label.

8. RegEdit will then import the user's Registry data.

9. Once you have reviewed or made your changes, highlight the Hive and select the Unload Hive option from the File menu.

Figure 4-1. Loading NTuser.dat in RegEdit

To load the same Hive directly into RegEdit, type the following command, with the username of the account you want to load the Hive for, into an elevated Command Prompt or administrative PowerShell console:

```
reg.exe load HKLM\TommyLee "c:\users\Tommy Lee\ntuser.dat"
```

■ **Note**   You are only able to use RegEdit to access the HKEY_USERS and HKEY_LOCAL_MACHINE Hives from another user.

The system hides NTuser files by default, so you may need to amend your Folder Options settings within File Explorer to enable the viewing of hidden system files.

If you do not have third-party tools available and you want to compare two registries side by side, you can use the following command in an administrative PowerShell console to open an additional, separate instance of RegEdit:

```
Regedit.exe –m
```

If you do not have an existing instance of RegEdit running, you will receive an error.

Once you have two instances of RegEdit running, if you are using Windows 7 or later you can use the Windows Snap feature to compare the results side by side, as shown in Figure 4-2.

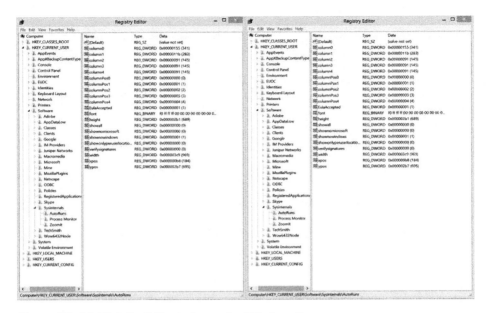

Figure 4-2. *Multiple RegEdit windows using Windows Snap*

If you are not familiar with the Snap feature, you can use the keyboard shortcuts: Windows+left arrow to snap the window against the left side or Windows+right arrow to snap it against the right.

■ **Note** The Regedit.exe –m command will work with Windows XP and later OSs, and requires at least one instance of RegEdit already to be running.

Remote Administration

To activate Remote Administration on a PC there are several steps to go through. The first is to open the Group Policy Editor (search for gpedit.msc in the Start Menu search box or at the Start Screen) and navigate to Computer Configuration ➤ Administrative Templates ➤ Network ➤ Network Connections ➤ Firewall, and then either Domain Profile or Standard Profile depending on how you will connect to and manage the PC.

You will want to enable the Windows Firewall: Allow inbound remote administration exception. When you do this you will be informed (see Figure 4-3) that this will permit tools such as the Microsoft Management Console (MMC) and Windows Management Instrumentation (WMI) to remote-administer the PC.

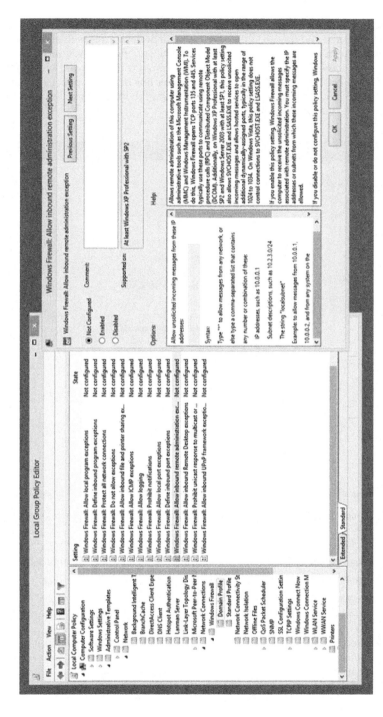

Figure 4-3. *Activating Remote Administration in the Group Policy Editor*

You will also be told to open TCP ports 135 and 445 in the firewall. To open the firewall, either search for Firewall in the Start Menu or at the Start Screen and, when it opens, click the Advanced Settings link in the left panel, or open the Administrative Tools from the Control Panel and you will see Windows Firewall with Advanced Security listed.

In the Advanced Firewall, click the Inbound Rules link in the left panel, then the New Rule... link in the right panel. You can now create a new inbound rule to permit access to ports 135 and 445 (see Figure 4-4).

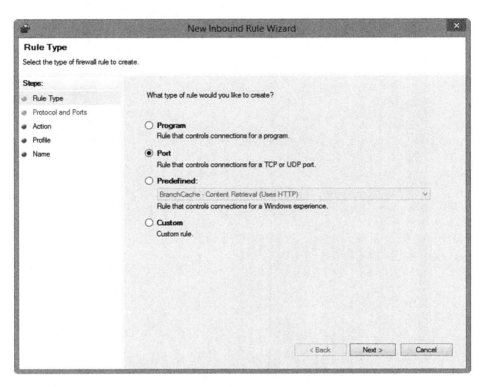

Figure 4-4. Opening a port in the Windows Firewall

■ **Note**   You can enable or disable the Remote Administration exception in Group Policy from the Command line by using the command `netsh firewall set service type = remoteadmin mode = [mode]` where [mode] is either `enable` or `disable`.

The last step is to activate the Remote Registry service on the PC you want to remotely administer. The Remote Registry Service can be found in the Windows Services panel, or you can search for `services.msc` in the Start Menu search box or at the Start Screen (see Figure 4-5).

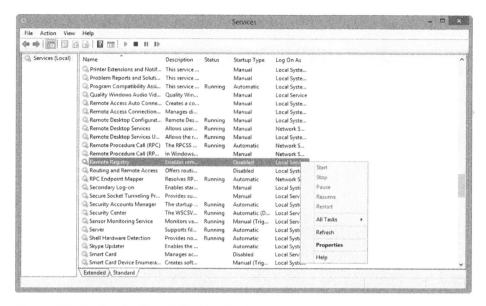

Figure 4-5. *Starting the Remote Registry Service*

To activate the service, right-click and select Properties from the context menu that appears. The service is disabled by default but a dialog will appear where you can enable and start the service.

■ **Note**   To enable and start the Remote Registry service from the Command Prompt, type sc start RemoteRegistry. You can set it to automatically start each time the computer boots using the command sc config RemoteRegistry start = auto.

Connecting to a Remote Registry

For information to be polled from a target PC you must first ensure that the Remote Registry Service is enabled and running, as shown in Figure 4-6.

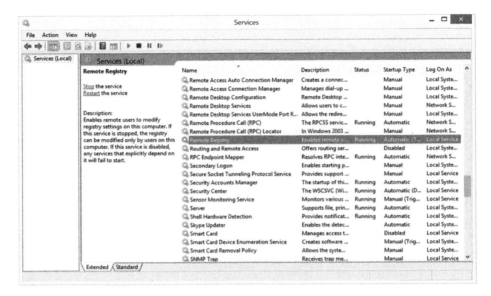

Figure 4-6. *Enabling the Remote Registry Service*

With the Remote Registry Service running on both the local and remote PCs, you can then attempt to connect across the network from within RegEdit:

1. Log on to your computer as an administrator.

2. Type RegEdit at the Start Screen and press Enter.

3. Accept the UAC warning.

4. Click File and select Connect Network Registry

5. Enter the name of the PC you wish to connect to. You can also click the Advanced button and then click Find Now to list all available PCs on the network that you can connect to.

6. Click OK.

7. You will now see the PC listed and two new branches appear within RegEdit: one for HKLU and one for HKU.

8. Once you have reviewed or made your changes, highlight the Computer icon and select the Disconnect Network Registry option from the File menu.

If you prefer to use the command line rather than the GUI tools, you can use the following commands to enable and start the Remote Registry Service, respectively:

```
sc config remoteregistry start=demand
```

```
net start remoteregistry
```

Windows PowerShell

PowerShell does not natively allow the manipulation of the Registry on a remote PC. This could be achieved through some coding to create a script with the .NET Framework (using the `Microsoft.Win32.Registry` and `Microsoft.Win32.RegistryKey` classes), but this is outside of the scope of this book.

In Chapter 2 we explored how PowerShell could be used to configure Registry settings with Group Policy Preferences, which can be directed at remote PCs and users in an organization.

Using Group Policy Preferences

Enterprise administrators may have to maintain thousands of PCs and servers within their organization. Manually configuring changes to each PC would be very time consuming and error prone. Group Policy is a feature of Microsoft's popular Active Directory Directory Services (AD DS), which allows resources such as user accounts, groups, PCs, and servers to be managed centrally.

Group Policy Preferences (GPPs) were introduced with the Windows XP Group Policy Preference Client Side Extensions. They added the ability for an administrator to deploy and modify Registry settings to multiple PCs and servers within the organization easily. Registry settings are only one of the types of settings that GPPs allow administrators to maintain. This section will provide you with some insight and guidance for using GPPs to deploy and modify Registry settings in your own environment.

If you are signed into a domain-joined PC and have and account with administrative credentials, you will be able to use the Remote Server Administration Tools (RSAT) to manage AD DS from your PC. Alternatively you can open a console connection to the server (if permitted) using the Remote Desktop Protocol (RDP) and use the AD DS tools interactively.

Download the version of RSAT that you need from from the Microsoft web site. There are different versions of RSAT for different versions of Windows, so you should search for the one you need.

Using your PC or the server, you will now take a look at the GPPs and how they can be used to manage Registry settings within the enterprise:

1. Using either a PC with RSAT installed or a RDP console to the server, open the Group Policy Management Console (GPMC).

2. Right-click Group Policy Objects (GPOs) and select New, then provide the GPO a name such as ModifySoftware.

3. Right-click the ModifySoftware GPO, and select Edit.

4. Expand Computer Configuration ➤ Preferences ➤ Windows Settings and then double-click the Registry icon.

5. Right-click Registry and select New as shown in Figure 4-7.

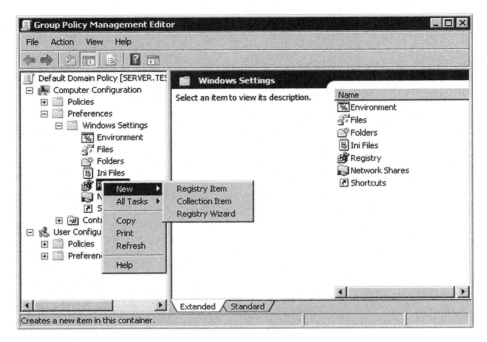

Figure 4-7. *Creating new Registry keys with Group Policy Preferences*

There are three Registry key options available to choose from, as shown in Table 4-1.

Table 4-1. *Options for Creating New Registry Keys with Group Policy Preferences*

New Option	Description
Registry Item	Allows creation of a single Registry item.
Collection Item	Creates and organizes Registry Preference items into a folder. Useful if you need to add a group of Registry items.
Registry Wizard	Wizard to use the local Registry as a reference, or connect to a remote PC. Allows creation of single or multiple entries.

1. Choose the Registry Wizard.

2. Browse to the required location and configure the required keys and values to import into the GPPs.

3. Click Finish.

4. Expand the Registry entries and review as shown in Figure 4-8.

5. By default the Action is set to Update.

Figure 4-8. *Setting the Action condition within Group Policy Preferences*

There are four Action options available to choose from, as shown in Table 4-2.

Table 4-2. *Action Conditions Available Within Group Policy Preferences*

Available Action	Description
Create	• Creates the Registry item • Ignored if the item exists
Update (Default)	• If the item already exists, it will be updated • It the item does not exist, it will be created
Replace	• Delete the existing item if it already exists and create a new item
Delete	• Deletes the item

1. Once you have reviewed the options, click OK.

2. Link the GPO to an Organizational Unit to enable it.

3. Close the GPMC.

■ **Note** When you run Group Policy on your local machine, you are using Local Group Policy, which does not contain Group Policy Preferences. GPPs can be managed from systems with the GPP Client Side Extensions. These extensions need to be separately downloaded for Windows XP and Windows Server 2003, but are available as a built-in feature that you can enable on client PCs running Windows Vista with Service Pack 1 (or later) with the RSAT or Windows Server 2008 (or later).

Comparing Registries

We have already mentioned that nearly everything that is installed or configured on a Windows PC is stored within the Registry. During a typical software installation you will be surprised by the scale of how much Registry activity occurs. Often tens of thousands of Registry keys are added or edited during even a relatively small software installation. If we were able to compare the Registry of a PC before and after one of these events, we would be able to see the changes made within the Registry.

We can use special utilities to effectively take snapshots of the Registry, before and after these events, so that we can make a comparison between two exported files. Another forensic technique is to compare registries from one machine and a different or reference PC to identify the changes that are in effect between the two PCs. Some Registry comparison tools are listed in Table 4-3.

Table 4-3. *Popular Third-Party Registry Compare Utilities*

Tool	Download URL
File Compare (`fc.exe`)	Included in Windows XP
InstallWatch Pro	`http://installwatch-pro.en.lo4d.com/`
Process Monitor (Windows Sysinternals)	`http://technet.microsoft.com/sysinternals/bb896645.aspx`
Regshot	`www.aplusfreeware.com/categories/util/registry.html`
Tiny Watcher	`http://kubicle.dcmembers.com/watcher/`
Total Commander	`http://ghisler.com/`
What Changed	`www.majorgeeks.com/files/details/what_changed.html`
WinDiff	`www.grigsoft.com/download-windiff.htm`
WinMerge	`http://winmerge.org`

Advanced Troubleshooting

All of the repair methods for the Windows Registry that we've detailed so far rely on the OS being in a state in which it will either boot, or the startup options will work. What should you do, though, if the Registry is so corrupt that neither of these is an option? Do you need to reinstall the OS from an image backup or can the Registry still be repaired?

The former option is often seen as the quick and simple way for a systems administrator to fix a problem, but it's rarely as quick and simple as might first appear. Yes, you can restore a Windows system image in less than the 30 minutes—normally deemed "the holy grail" of repair times, especially in a enterprise environment—but most PCs will very likely then have a huge number of Windows, software, and other updates to install, not to mention any configuration or user changes that were made after the backup image was created.

All of these things can add an extra couple of hours to the repair time for a PC, during which the machine itself, and the person relying on it, is unproductive. Tools do exist to help you repair the Registry in case of a full-on crisis, however, and some careful planning and preparation can help get even an unbootable Windows installation working again.

Running RegEdit from Windows Installation Media

One of the ironies about the Windows operating system is that as the OS has become more stable, reliable, and robust, the amount of tools and utilities available to repair it has expanded in number and functionality. Your Windows installation media also contains these tools, such as System Restore, mentioned in Chapter 3.

You can also access RegEdit by booting from your Windows installation media. The process for doing this will vary slightly depending on the Windows version you are using.

Booting into the Recovery Options in Vista and Windows 7

If you are repairing a Windows Vista or Windows 7 installation, click through the language choice when starting the PC from your installation media and, at the Install screen, click the Repair your computer link. This will likely, but not always, launch System Image Repair and you'll need to get out of this.

Check the option to Restore your computer using a system image that you created earlier and click Next. It's likely that no additional images will be found, but either way at the next dialog you're presented with Re-image your computer. Click Cancel to access the Windows Recovery options (see Figure 4-9).

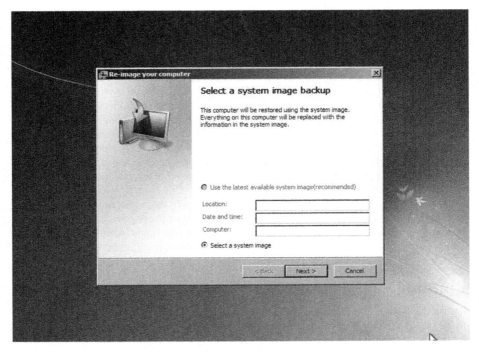

Figure 4-9. *Accessing the Recovery Options in Windows Vista and Windows 7*

When the System Recovery Options appear, open the Command Prompt, and it's here that you can type RegEdit.exe to start RegEdit.

Booting into the Recovery Options in Windows 8 and Windows 8.1

Starting a PC from installation media in Windows 8 and Windows 8.1 can be trickier, because the OS starts so quickly that there's not time enough in which to press F8 to display the boot options menu.

You can access the PC's BIOS/UEFI system and change the boot order if need be, and how you do this will vary from one PC to another, but it's more likely at this point that Windows won't start at all, so you should boot fine from the installation media.

At the first options screen click the Troubleshoot option, and then Advanced Options at the next screen. You will now see a Command Prompt button to click (see Figure 4-10), and it's here that you can type RegEdit.exe to start RegEdit.

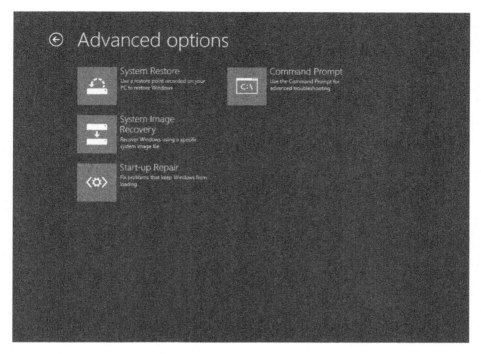

Figure 4-10. *Accessing RegEdit from Windows 8 and 8.1 installation media*

Using RegEdit from the Recovery Environment

RegEdit, when run from Windows installation media, or indeed from a system recovery disk or USB recovery drive, won't be connected to the Registry files for Windows on your hard disk, nor will they be attached to the Registry files for any user account on the PC. Instead, you will be looking directly at the Registry for the installation media itself, and yes, it does have one; see Figure 4-11.

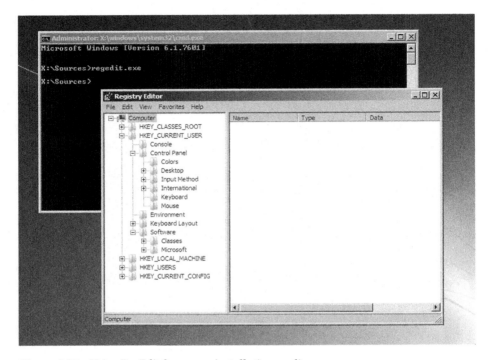

Figure 4-11. *Using RegEdit from your installation media*

You will thus need to connect RegEdit to the appropriate file or files you want to work on. This is done in the Administrative Command Prompt before you open RegEdit itself, and was detailed at the beginning of this chapter.

You will connect to a user's Registry files using the command reg.exe load HKLM\ TommyLee "c:\users\Tommy Lee\ntuser.dat", but you may want to change the name and location of the .dat file to one of the core OS Registry files located in the %systemroot%\System 32\Config\ folder of the hard disk, as detailed in Chapter 1.

Once connected to the appropriate Registry file, you can make changes in the same way as if you were using RegEdit on a working PC, including importing a backup copy of an old Registry file if this is required.

Repairing the Registry using a Portable OS

Windows Vista introduced a system called Shadow Copy, which allows backups to be made of core operating system files while they're still in use. This allows you to add the core Registry files to your standard regular backup. You do have one, right?

Optionally, when you create a System Image of the OS you may choose to create backup copies of the Registry manually within RegEdit itself. Bear in mind, however, that restoring an older copy of a full Registry to a Windows installation that has had OS, software, and driver updates and changes will inevitably create a situation where some components will be unstable or nonfunctional.

■ **Note**   A quick note on the System Volume Information folder, which System Restore uses to make periodic backup copies of system files, including the Registry: these files are stored in a compressed and encrypted *.dat file container and cannot be accessed for reasons of security and to prevent malware infection.

This brings us back to adding your PC's Registry files to your regular backup. Armed with these files you can start your PC from a portable OS such as GNU/Linux, Ubuntu (as shown in Figure 4-12), or a USB-bootable copy of Windows and restore those Registry files using the file explorer in the portable OS. This will allow you to display all files, though bear in mind you will likely need to check the relevant option to show all hidden files on the hard disk.

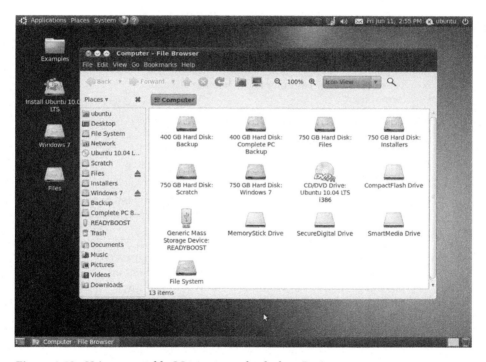

Figure 4-12. *Using a portable OS to restore a backed-up Registry*

■ **Note**   You cannot use a Windows To Go USB Flash Drive to access the file system on the host computer, as it is blocked for security reasons.

Creating a Portable Windows OS USB Flash Drive

It is possible to create a bootable Windows 7, Windows 8, or Windows 8.1 USB flash drive, containing all your software without requiring Windows To Go. This can be useful if you do not have access to an Enterprise edition of Windows 8 or 8.1 (Windows 7 did not support Windows To Go).

You will need a spare license for the copy of Windows you install on the USB flash drive, but it has the advantage of being able to let you view all the folders and files on the host PC.

To create a portable Windows installation you will need an install DVD or ISO file.

1. Open the Command Prompt (Admin) from within Windows on the desktop.

2. Type diskpart and press Enter.

3. Type list disk and press Enter. This displays a list of disks in your PC. Make a note of the number for the USB flash drive (1, 2, etc.).

4. Type select disk n, where n represents the disk number for your USB flash drive.

5. Type clean and press Enter to prepare the drive for formatting.

6. Type create partition primary and press Enter.

7. Type format fs=ntfs quick and press Enter.

8. Type active and press Enter to make the newly created partition the active (bootable) partition.

9. Type assign letter=e and press Enter, to temporarily assign a drive letter to the flash drive so you can install Windows onto it.

10. Type Exit and press Enter to exit Diskpart.

11. Now place your Windows installation DVD into your DVD drive or mount your ISO image as a drive. You can mount ISO images natively in Windows 8 and Windows 8.1 by right-clicking them and selecting Mount from the options that appear. In Windows 7 you will need a third-party utility such as WinISO.

12. Back at the Command Prompt type dism /apply-image /imagefile=f:\sources\install.wim /index:1 /applydir:e:\ where f is the location of your ISO file or DVD and e is the USB flash drive. This will copy the Windows installer image to the flash drive and takes around 8GB of space.

13. Type bcdboot.exe e:\Windows /s e: /f ALL to set the USB flash drive as being bootable.

You can now boot your PC from the flash drive, but note that you may need to change the boot setting in the BIOS/UEFI for this, and use this portable OS to repair the host PC. The initial setup process for the flash drive when you first start the PC from it can take some time, and it's a good idea to do this on the PC you intend to repair, as moving the drive between different PCs—especially with different BIOS/UEFI types—can result in the flash drive not working on some machines or Windows believing the hardware it has been installed on has changed, and asking for a fresh product key.

■ **Note** If you intend to use this flash drive for a one-time repair, Windows 7 presents a good option, as it offers a 30-day trial of the OS. You can download a trial of the current Windows version from the TechNet Evaluation Center at `http://technet.microsoft.com/en-gb/evalcenter`.

One last point to note is that you can repair any version of Windows by using any other version of Windows as a portable OS. It is, for example, perfectly okay to repair Windows 10 using a Windows 7 bootable Flash Drive. The two operating systems won't be in a dual-boot system, and so long as one can read the file system of the other all will work well. This won't work with drives that are encrypted with BitLocker Drive Encryption, however, where you will need to resort to a System Image recovery.

Repair the Registry Without Booting Windows

Everyone likes a new tool or program, and I recall a Microsoft trainer friend explaining to me one day how she had used a tool called Autoruns—another utility from the Sysinternals Suite. She decided that the userinit.exe listed on her Windows XP machine was spyware, and deleted the item from the list in Autoruns. Not such a great idea, because once she rebooted her PC and tried to log on, the machine automatically logged off again. Somehow, she had removed a crucial setting within the Registry and could not gain access to the Registry (or Autoruns) to fix the problem.

We have discussed several ways in which a modern operating system can recover from a scenario like this one, but my favorite is still System Restore. There are several third-party tools that will help fix Windows problems prior to Windows loading—these are especially useful for systems running an OS prior to Windows 8.1 as they allow booting direct from a CD or DVD. Recovery tools that allow you to access the Registry from outside of Windows include the following:

- PCRegEdit

- Hiren's Boot CD

- Lazesoft Recovery Suite Home—Recovery CD

- UBCD4Win

- DaRT—part of the Microsoft Desktop Optimization Pack for Software Assurance (MDOP)

We will walk through the steps to recover the preceding case study by using the popular Hiren's Boot CD.

1. Download the Hiren's Boot CD ISO.

2. Create a bootable USB or CD from Hirensbootcd.iso.

3. Boot the PC with the Hiren disk, then select Mini Windows XP.

4. Allow Mini XP to load, then click the Hiren menu icon and select Registry, then Registry Editor PE.

5. Set the remote Windows directory to C:\Windows and click OK.

6. To edit the Registry Hive HKEY_CURRENT_USER, you need to load NTUSER.DAT from the User directory.

7. Expand HKEY_LOCAL_MACHINE and navigate to _REMOTE_SOFTWARE\Microsoft\Windows NT\ CurrentVersion\Winlogon.

8. Edit the Userinit key and set the value to "C:\Windows\System32\Userinit.exe" as shown in Figure 4-13.

9. When you close RegEdit the Hives will automatically unload and you can then exit the Hiren's toolkit and reboot the PC.

Figure 4-13. *Editing the Userinit key within RegEdit*

Summary

With PCs being designed to maximize the potential for multi-user environments, it might seem perplexing that it's often difficult to edit and troubleshoot the Registry files for user accounts other than your own. As you have seen in this chapter, however, it can be achieved without too much fuss.

The primary reason for Microsoft making it difficult, however, is to maintain a high level of security for both the Registry and the PC, and it's maximizing your Registry's security that we'll talk about in the next chapter.

■ ■ ■

CHAPTER 5

Securing the Registry

As a parent, I was once told that if children are left to play, then they will happily play all day without getting themselves into any trouble, but if a door or garden gate is forgetfully left open, then children will wander, explore, begin to get into mischief. . . . There are many doors in the Registry, but while some may be opened, thankfully Windows will protect us from destroying the Registry. On a modern operating system, the Windows security model is very robust and will do a very good job at protecting itself from destruction, sometimes despite our own best endeavors to undermine security.

As you discovered earlier, a PC is only secure if Windows does not get compromised. Windows can be attacked from many vectors, and we will highlight a few in this chapter to help prevent unauthorized access to your system and ultimately the Registry. We have identified several areas where an attacker can seek to gain access to your system. These include:

- Physical security

- Anti-malware

- User protection

- Encryption

- Password security

Physical Security—Locking the Door

We have learned that a defense-in-depth approach to security is the best way to protect our systems. That is, we should protect the heart of the system by building up layers of defenses to either thwart attackers or to slow and discourage them during their attack so that they are motivated to move on to an easier target. In this section we offer a number of recommendations that can be applied specifically to securing the Registry.

Disable the Remote Registry Service

You saw in Chapter 4 that to enable remote administration of the Registry, you must enable the Remote Registry Service. To prevent unauthorized access to your Registry across the network, you should ensure that the Remote Registry Service is disabled and not running (by default it is set to Disabled), as shown in Figure 5-1.

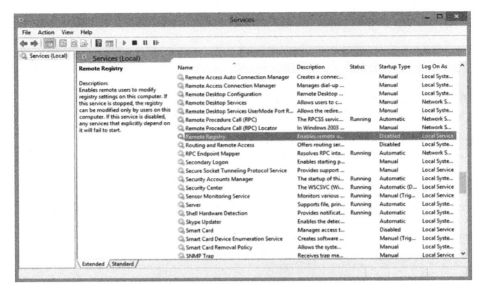

Figure 5-1. *Ensuring the Remote Registry Service is disabled*

Restrict Remote Users

Members of the special Remote Management Users group are given the necessary group membership rights to be allowed to manage the PC remotely. In Windows 8, you should review the built-in Remote Management Users group membership and ensure that only the user accounts that you approve are listed. Remove any user accounts and user groups that should not have access as shown in Figure 5-2.

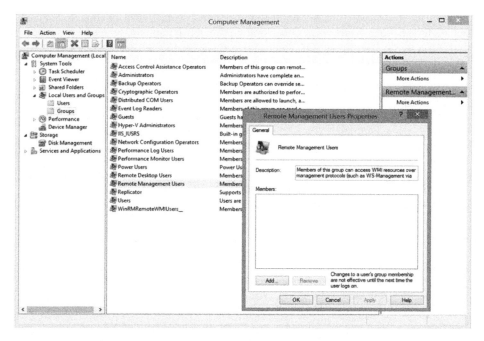

Figure 5-2. *Configuring Remote Management Users Group membership*

Windows 7 provides remote access to only administrators of the machine, whereas in Windows 8 members of the Remote Users Group are also granted remote access to the machine.

Driver Signature Enforcement

In Windows 8, all device drivers are digitally signed, which guarantees that the driver has not been tampered with. This should reassure us that the driver is safeguarded against being infected with malware.

A signed driver, however, is not a guarantee that it will be compatible with your hardware. As we have already discussed in Chapter 3, drivers are allowed to write information directly into the Registry, and badly written drivers have been known to have caused system failures especially when installed on Windows XP and Windows Vista devices.

Driver signing is a good way to protect a system from rogue, poorly written, or infected driver software. Unfortunately the appreciation of what driver signing means is seldom understood, especially by non-technical people.

Drivers remain an essential commodity for the PC owner and an area that attracts a lot of attention from people with unscrupulous intent. You only need to search for a driver on the Internet to find dozens of websites offering to provide you with drivers that, unknown to the user, will include additional software that infects your PC with ransomware or spyware. Both of these activities fool thousands of people daily and this "business" is now worth millions of dollars annually.

In case you are still unsure whether an unsigned driver is cause for concern, let us delve a little deeper. Windows has been built to run in two main modes—a kernel mode and a user mode. User mode runs applications and software on a top layer of Windows and interacts continuously with the operating system, but never directly controls system resources, RAM, CPU, or hard drives.

Kernel mode is a trusted area. Windows gives full access to the internal memory spaces and does not regulate, check, or provide any protection to the system from components that are trusted to run in kernel mode. Internal Windows processes, including system code such as services and device drivers, run completely within kernel mode. It is therefore vital that these components be carefully designed and tested, because once they have access to run in kernel mode they completely bypass Windows security to access objects on the system.

To list all drivers that have been registered on a PC, you can use the built-in Msinfo32.exe utility in Windows.

1. Search for Msinfo32 on the Start screen in Windows 8.1 or in the Start Menu in Windows 7.

2. Select the System Drivers entry under Software Environment.

3. Sort the drivers by the Started column; drivers that are loaded are represented by a "Yes" in Figure 5-3.

	Name	Description	File	Type	Started	Start Mode	State	Status
System Summary	acpi	Microsoft ACPI Driver	c:\windo...	Kernel Driver	Yes	Boot	Running	OK
⊞ Hardware Resources	acpiex	Microsoft ACPIEx Driver	c:\windo...	Kernel Driver	Yes	Boot	Running	OK
⊞ Components	afd	Ancillary Function Driver fo...	c:\windo...	Kernel Driver	Yes	System	Running	OK
⊟ Software Environment	ahcache	Application Compatibility ...	c:\windo...	Kernel Driver	Yes	System	Running	OK
System Drivers	basicdisplay	BasicDisplay	c:\windo...	Kernel Driver	Yes	System	Running	OK
Environment Variables	basicrender	BasicRender	c:\windo...	Kernel Driver	Yes	System	Running	OK
Print Jobs	beep	Beep	c:\windo...	Kernel Driver	Yes	System	Running	OK
Network Connections	bowser	Browser Support Driver	c:\windo...	File System Driver	Yes	Manual	Running	OK
Running Tasks	btha2dp	Bluetooth Stereo	c:\windo...	Kernel Driver	Yes	Manual	Running	OK
Loaded Modules	bthavrcptg	Bluetooth Audio/Video Re...	c:\windo...	Kernel Driver	Yes	Manual	Running	OK
Services	bthenum	Bluetooth Enumerator Servi...	c:\windo...	Kernel Driver	Yes	Manual	Running	OK
Program Groups	bthhfaud	Bluetooth Hands-Free	c:\windo...	Kernel Driver	Yes	Manual	Running	OK
Startup Programs	bthhfenum	Bluetooth Hands-Free Audi...	c:\windo...	Kernel Driver	Yes	Manual	Running	OK
OLE Registration	bthhfhid	Bluetooth Hands-Free Call ...	c:\windo...	Kernel Driver	Yes	Manual	Running	OK
Windows Error Report	bthleenum	Bluetooth Low Energy Driver	c:\windo...	Kernel Driver	Yes	Manual	Running	OK
	bthpan	Bluetooth Device (Personal ...	c:\windo...	Kernel Driver	Yes	Manual	Running	OK
	bthusb	Bluetooth Radio USB Driver	c:\windo...	Kernel Driver	Yes	Manual	Running	OK
	clfs	Common Log (CLFS)	c:\windo...	Kernel Driver	Yes	Boot	Running	OK
	cmbatt	Microsoft ACPI Control Met...	c:\windo...	Kernel Driver	Yes	Manual	Running	OK
	cng	CNG	c:\windo...	Kernel Driver	Yes	Boot	Running	OK
	compositebus	Composite Bus Enumerator...	c:\windo...	Kernel Driver	Yes	Manual	Running	OK
	condrv	Console Driver	c:\windo...	Kernel Driver	Yes	Manual	Running	OK
	csc	Offline Files Driver	c:\windo...	Kernel Driver	Yes	System	Running	OK
	dfsc	DFS Namespace Client Driv...	c:\windo...	File System Driver	Yes	System	Running	OK
	disk	Disk Driver	c:\windo...	Kernel Driver	Yes	Boot	Running	OK
	dxgkrnl	LDDM Graphics Subsystem	c:\windo...	Kernel Driver	Yes	Manual	Running	OK
	exfat	exFAT File System Driver	c:\windo...	File System Driver	Yes	Manual	Running	OK
	fastfat	FAT12/16/32 File System D...	c:\windo...	File System Driver	Yes	Manual	Running	OK

Figure 5-3. Using Msinfo32.exe to view loaded drivers

You can also view the list of loaded kernel-mode drivers with Process Explorer, another tool in the Sysinternals suite.

The pop-up warning that a user receives when they attempt to load an unsigned third-party driver is often ignored, yet this is potentially one of the most common points of entry into a system that malware can adopt.

■ **Note**   There is no way to turn off the "unsigned driver" pop-up warnings in Windows on a permanent basis.

Restrict Physical Access

It may sound bizarre, but the majority of cyberattacks are carried out in person—interactively, from inside the enterprise, at an unattended PC or using a stolen laptop. Users should always lock their PCs when they leave their workstations, and devices should be configured to require a password whenever they resume from sleep or hibernation.

Windows 8 allows the PC to be locked manually by the user, or to lock automatically based on system inactivity, as shown in Figure 5-4. Within an enterprise environment administrators can also set this criteria by using Group Policy.

Figure 5-4. Windows 8 lock screen

In addition to using a lock screen, Windows employs an additional security feature that requires the user to click or hit any key to expose the login screen from the lock screen as shown in Figure 5-5.

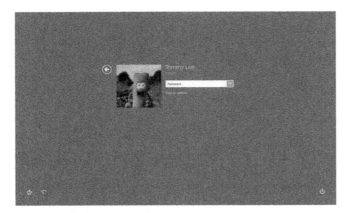

Figure 5-5. *Windows 8 interactive login screen*

Anti-Malware: Location, Location, Location

Windows has suffered greatly due to malware. The infection rate is significantly more prevalent on older operating systems, where users routinely signed in using administrative credentials (especially home and workgroup users) and allowed malware programs such as viruses, spyware, and Trojans to create entries within the Registry, which then allowed the malware access to the heart of their PCs.

PCs in home and workgroup settings continue to be affected to a greater extent than PCs in enterprise settings. Typically an enterprise user is provided with a preconfigured, managed device which is pretty much "locked down," and operators will not have the necessary permissions to install additional software. Only the IT team and helpdesk members will be able to add or remove software, and often this is controlled centrally by using Group Policy. By default users are members of the Standard Users group, which prevents them from making modifications to their PCs. In some situations, even the user profile is fixed by using mandatory profiles—another method of restricting the human interaction with the system Registry.

Members of a workgroup or HomeGroup in a peer-to-peer network—very popular in small and micro businesses with up to 10 PCs—are often configured to share multiple resources such as files, folders, and printers. This small shared network can provide an ideal environment for sharing software, which often leads to malware infestation that can quickly spread across the network.

The users of non-managed PCs are most at risk from Registry corruption and malware infestation, and they are also the least knowledgable about their vulnerability. Users in this group install software from a variety of sources, and in much greater frequency, often downloaded from torrent sites or file-sharing repositories. Typically a home and micro business user will utilize the administrator account as their normal user account and will ignore security warnings and UAC prompts designed to prevent unauthorized software installation such as malware (which often hitches a ride with freeware or shareware).

Windows 8 and 8.1 include a built-in anti-malware package called Windows
Defender, which is available as an optional download for Windows 7, where it's called
Security Essentials. This package forms the central internal defense for Windows
against virus, malware, and spyware attacks, though it also relies on additional Windows
components such as SmartScreen. So long as the software is running, and you have
Windows Updates enabled, your PC will be protected and Windows Defender will
monitor your system for issues in real time, as shown in Figure 5-6.

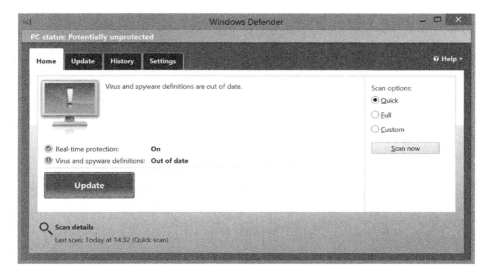

Figure 5-6. *Windows Defender status*

To confirm that your anti-malware signatures are current and that Windows
Defender is configured to operate in the background and perform real-time scanning,
perform the following steps:

1.   Type defender into the Start Screen and press Enter.

2.   Windows Defender will open.

3.   Review the Real-time protection status (on/off).

4.   Review the status of the virus and spyware definitions.

5.   If necessary click Update.

6.   Close Windows Defender.

Because Microsoft is able to update malware signatures via Windows Update quickly
to millions of PCs around the globe, Windows PCs are protected against the constant
threat of malware.

Enterprise customers will often choose to configure PCs within their organization
to receive enterprise-level anti-malware software updates, which allows greater
management capabilities such as deployment, reporting, and isolation-based quarantine.

The introduction of UAC has greatly reduced the infection rate from malware, although malware has also continued to advance and keeps finding new and innovative ways to infect our PCs.

User Protection—User Account Control

We have mentioned UAC several times in this book, and we want to restate the importance of maintaining this feature in its default state. It does an excellent job at not only protecting the Registry, but also protecting the whole of Windows (see Figure 5-7).

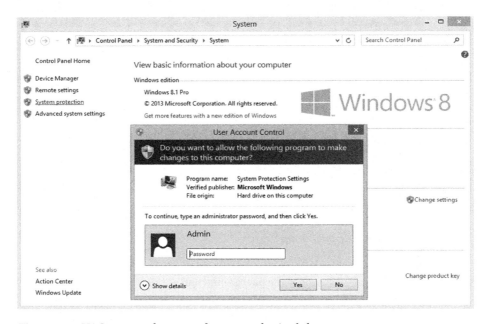

Figure 5-7. *UAC protects the system from unauthorized changes*

Most security breaches, malware, and Registry corruption is related to tasks carried out with administrator privileges—the most trusted status. Standard user accounts, on the other hand, are limited in their ability to make system-wide changes, and are even prevented from launching tools that could be used to make changes, such as allowing applications to be installed.

Some references mention UAC as a user protection tool, since it is aimed at protecting the system from the user, but unfortunately it is often ignored by the home and enthusiast PC owner. As mentioned, this ignorance is primarily due to a lack of awareness of what UAC actually does and how it helps with the defense-in-depth strategy that is absolutely required in the modern age of computing. Put bluntly, UAC is a key weapon against the constant and ever-changing threat from malware.

Educating users as to how UAC protects our systems is often overlooked. Within an enterprise, UAC will rarely present itself to typical users, since they are not routinely configuring, installing software on, or modifying their systems. These tasks are often the core roles for the IT support professionals to whom employees will turn, via the IT helpdesk, should they require changes to be made to their devices. IT support has the necessary administrative privileges, tools, and knowledge to respond to both the UAC prompt and the user's requested change.

We have mentioned that most PC users outside of the enterprise space are often configured as the administrator of the PC. For home and enthusiast users of Windows, the UAC has often been referred to as mildly annoying. Research has proven that over a period of time, a constant prompt by the UAC will become counterproductive, with users ignoring the warning presented and instead acknowledging the request to elevate, and that they see the UAC as simply a hurdle to cross in order to implement the change that the user initiated.

The main purpose of UAC, however, is not to annoy users. In Windows 8, thankfully, there were some slight changes to the way in which UAC interacts with the user. This fine tuning is certainly welcome, but it may be more appreciated by new users of Windows, who have not been frustrated by UAC since its introduction in Windows Vista.

To modify the UAC settings as shown in Figure 5-8, type UAC into the Start screen and press Enter or select Change User Account Control settings.

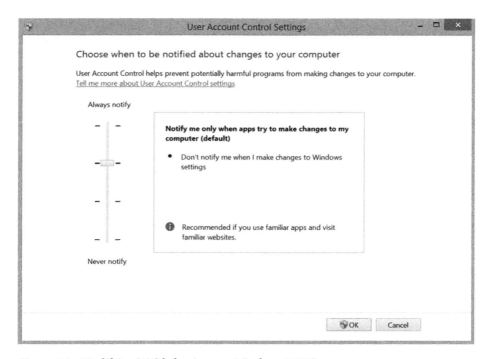

Figure 5-8. *Modifying UAC behavior on a Windows 8.1 PC*

Standard user accounts can be used to perform the following tasks:

- Burn CD/DVD media

- Change the desktop background

- Change the time zone

- Change their own user account password

- Configure accessibility options

- Configure power options

- Connect to a WiFi or LAN connection

- Install drivers, either from Windows Update or those that are supplied with Windows

- Install updates from Windows Update

- Modify their display settings

- Pair and configure a Bluetooth device with the PC

- Perform other troubleshooting and network diagnostic and repair tasks

- Play CD/DVD media

- Restore own files from File History

- Use Remote Desktop to connect to another PC

- View most settings, although they will require elevated permissions when attempting to change Windows settings

Administrators have a great amount of power—they can read, write, execute and modify all resources and Windows permissions on a PC.

One of the most noticeable aspects of UAC is that even an administrator is required to operate routinely with standard user–level permissions. Only when they attempt to carry out an administrative task will Windows prompt them with the UAC pop-up as shown in Figure 5-9, requiring that they acknowledge that the task requires administrative privileges to complete the operation (or cancel the operation). This principle is known as Admin Approval Mode.

Figure 5-9. *UAC Adminstrator approval request*

Table 5-1 shows the differences between the elevation prompts that each type of user will receive each time they wish to perform a task that will have system-wide impact.

Table 5-1. *UAC Elevation Prompt Types*

Elevation Prompt Type	Description
Consent	Only shown to administrators in Admin Approval Mode when they try to perform an administrative task
Credential	Shown to standard users when they attempt to perform an administrative task

Typical scenarios where a standard user would be prompted by UAC for the elevation to administrative privileges to complete the task include the following:

- Add or remove a user account
- Browse to another user's directory
- Change user account types
- Change Windows Firewall settings
- Configure Automatic Updates
- Configure Parental Controls
- Install a driver for a device
- Install ActiveX controls
- Install and uninstall applications
- Modify UAC settings

83

- Move or copy files into the Program Files or Windows directories

- Restore system backup files

- Schedule Automated Tasks

For users of Windows 8.1 and later, it is not possible to actually turn off UAC—it is an integral part of the modern operating system security model. It is possible to silence the notifications by moving the slider shown in Figure 5-8 all the way down to the bottom (Never Notify).

Our best practice recommendation is to educate users on why the UAC prompts are designed to protect the operating system and to maintain UAC at the default setting.

Encryption—BitLocker

One of the trends of modern computing is that the majority of devices have become increasingly mobile. This is great for scenarios that benefit from mobility, but the downside is the increased number of devices that get left on a train, stolen, or accidentally dropped and damaged. During 2013 in the UK alone, over 880,000 devices were stolen or lost.

Most devices that are lost or stolen are resold on the black market to unsuspecting (or not) purchasers, and the device then has a second life. Some theft is much more sinister and results in the device being stolen to order, with the aim of gaining corporate network entry or access to data contained on the device.

The majority of laptop owners rely entirely on the username/password combination that they type into the PC offering them protection against unauthorized access to their corporate data or (for home users) personal information. This process utilizes the NTLM protocol to securely authenticate and is an excellent, proven method of security.

Yet most users are unaware (and shocked to learn when told) that simply removing the hard drive from a lost, stolen, or damaged laptop and connecting it to another computer will allow anyone with administrative privileges on the local PC to read and extract all the information contained on the hard drive without any special skills, tools, or passwords, thus completely bypassing the built-in Windows security.

Third-party drive encryption software to help protect against this method of data access has been available for many years. Microsoft provided BitLocker Drive Encryption, a tool available since Windows Vista, which has allowed users and enterprises to completely encrypt the hard drive on their PCs—thereby preventing unauthorized access to their data, even if the drive is lost and subjected to the process just outlined. BitLocker is an encryption-based technology that works "under the hood" of Windows to ensure that the device is secure even *before* Windows takes over.

Still, despite BitLocker and similar tools being available, only a tiny proportion of devices are actually encrypted by their owners. With the release of Windows 8.1 and later, Microsoft has enabled BitLocker device encryption on all OEM-shipped devices by default. Once the new owner of the device signs on to the device using their Microsoft account, the BitLocker encryption is completed and the BitLocker recovery keys are automatically stored within the user's own OneDrive location (formerly known as SkyDrive), which is available by signing on to the page at https://onedrive.live.com/recoverykey.

BitLocker is an extremely secure way of protecting your Windows device. It encrypts all of the key files on the computer including the operating system, the Registry, hibernation, paging files, and all the user data, information programs, and settings on the encrypted disk drive.

The key required by BitLocker to grant access to the data is stored within a special tamperproof microchip on the motherboard of the device, called a Trusted Platform Module (TPM) chip. TPM chips were quite rare as little as five years ago, but now they are commonplace and required as part of the official Microsoft software and hardware certification program. The majority of systems available today support TPM versions 1.2 or 2.

The TPM is a hardware device that BitLocker can use to securely store the AES 128-bit encryption keys. You can see if your device has a TPM chip and check the version number using the TPM Administration tool within Control Panel as shown in Figure 5-10.

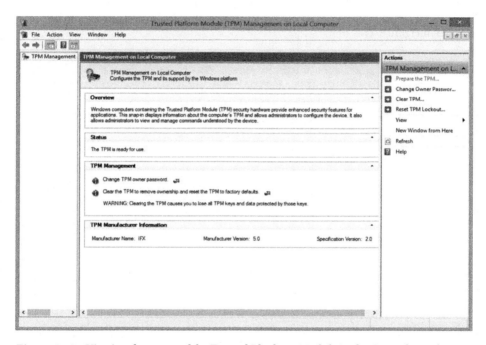

Figure 5-10. *Viewing the status of the Trusted Platform Module in the Control Panel*

How to determine if a PC has a TPM chip?

1. Open Control Panel, click System and Security, and then click BitLocker Drive Encryption.

2. Click TPM Administration.

3. The TPM Management on Local Computer Microsoft Management Console (MMC) appears.

4. Notice the message in the center of the MMC.

5. If the PC does not have a TPM, the "Compatible TPM cannot be found" message appears.

BitLocker can be enabled on devices even without a TPM chip, and unlocking these devices will require the user to type the unlock key, or provide a USB that contains the key.

In the earlier scenario where the disk drive has been removed from a device, the thief will be unable to extract any data from a BitLocker-encrypted drive because the drive must be unlocked by the TPM chip (or key). Otherwise the drive remains completely encrypted.

If the stolen device is able to boot, the data still remains protected by the normal Windows username/password logon prompt, which is also very secure.

If you are using a modern operating system you will be able to see if your device has a TPM chip, and the status of BitLocker Drive Encryption on your device, via the Control Panel item called BitLocker Drive Encryption within the System and Security section, as shown in Figure 5-11.

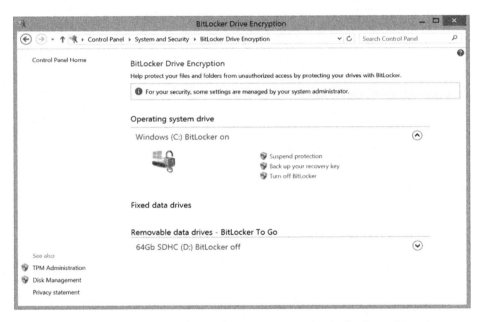

Figure 5-11. *Viewing the status of BitLocker Drive Encryption in the Control Panel*

In an enterprise environment, Windows 8 Pro and Windows 8 Enterprise editions can be managed by using Group Policy, and BitLocker recovery keys can be centralized in AD DS using a tool called Microsoft BitLocker Administration and Monitoring 2.5 (MBAM). MBAM provides the following management tasks:

- Deployment and recovery of encryption keys

- Centralized compliance monitoring and reporting

- Provisioning of encrypted drives

- Support for encrypted drives, including a self-service portal for users to recover their recovery keys

- Enforcement of organizational BitLocker policies

■ **Note**   Microsoft BitLocker Administration and Monitoring 2.5 is only available as part of the Microsoft Desktop Optimization Pack (MDOP), which is a benefit to Microsoft Software Assurance customers.

BitLocker Drive Encryption can be installed on different versions of Windows as shown in Table 5-2.

Table 5-2. *BitLocker Drive Encryption in Microsoft Windows Versions*

Windows Version	Edition	Description
Windows Vista	Ultimate and Enterprise	Allowed only system drive to be encrypted
Windows 7	Ultimate and Enterprise	Full GPO management ability, allows all drives to be encrypted
Windows 8	Pro and Enterprise	Full GPO management ability, allows all drives to be encrypted
Windows RT	RT	Device Encryption using BitLocker encryption
Windows 8.1	All	Device Encryption using BitLocker encryption. No management capability (on/off only).
Windows 8.1	Pro and Enterprise	Full GPO management ability, allows all drives to be encrypted

Although outside the scope of this book, BitLocker can also be deployed to protect removable drives such as SDHC cards, USB hard drives, and thumb drives using a feature called BitLocker To Go. Enterprises have the ability to allow or deny users the ability to save data onto external drives that are not BitLocker encrypted by using the extensive GPOs that are available.

■ **Note**   If you want to use BitLocker to protect a drive on a PC without a TPM, you must enable the Require additional authentication at startup policy setting within Group Policy, and then within that setting, click Allow BitLocker without a compatible TPM.

We hope that you can appreciate from this short introduction of BitLocker Drive Encryption that this feature is a valuable defensive strategy that protects against data theft. BitLocker encrypts entire volumes on a hard disk, making them unusable unless the drive has been unlocked by BitLocker, and thereby minimizes the risk of data loss on computers that are lost or stolen.

Password Security

Passwords have been at the heart of most computer system security for several decades, and while the protocols have improved, the concept has remained the same: a user will sign in to a PC using a username and password to gain access.

In this section we describe a free tool from Microsoft that will allow users and administrators to establish what level of security their machine exhibits, and will also highlight vulnerabilities and areas for concern. The tool scans the local PC (or even a whole network of PCs) for a multitude of security-related issues and displays the results in an easy-to-read and understand report.

The tool is called Microsoft Baseline Security Analyzer (MBSA) and can be downloaded at www.microsoft.com/en-gb/download/details.aspx?id=7558. The reason to include the tool in this section is because it will scan and report on the existence of weak passwords, and of computer accounts that may not have any passwords set at all! The tool has been available for download for over 10 years but rarely, during my onsite consultancy visits, do I encounter many enterprises using the tool.

Download MBSA and follow the wizard to run the security analysis on your PC. An example report is shown in Figure 5-12.

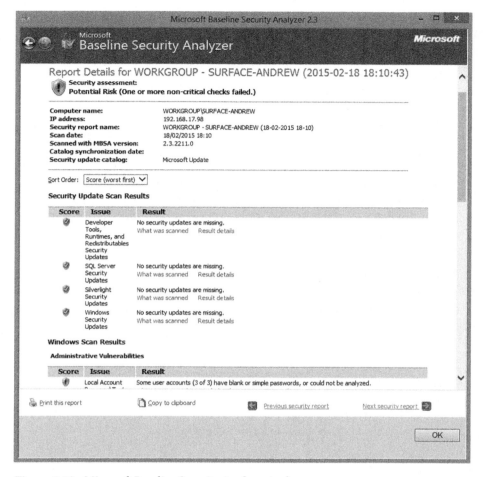

Figure 5-12. *Microsoft Baseline Security Analyzer tool*

MBSA will check for the following issues:

- Basic vulnerabilities

- Missing Windows Update patches

- Microsoft SQL Server vulnerabilities

- Internet Information Server (IIS) vulnerabilities

- Basic security settings and weaknesses

- Weak passwords

- Accounts with no passwords

- Status of the built-in guest account

Because of the nature of the scan, MBSA requires administrative privileges on the PCs that it is scanning.

■ **Note**   You can also use MBSA to perform security scans on servers.

We are particularly interested in finding the existence of weak or no passwords on the systems. For passwords to be effective, they should be strong and changed on a regular basis, such as every 60 days. The definition of a strong password in Microsoft's security policy is as follows:

- Not contain the user's account name or parts of the user's full name that exceed two consecutive characters

- Be at least six characters in length

- Contain characters from *three* of the following four categories:

  - English uppercase characters (A through Z)

  - English lowercase characters (a through z)

  - Base 10 digits (0 through 9)

  - Non-alphabetic characters (e.g., !, $, #, %)

- Complexity requirements are enforced when passwords are changed or created.

The password policy can be set via Group Policy or on the local computer via the Local Group Policy Editor. To open the Local Group Policy Editor type secpol.msc into the Start Screen in Windows 8 or 8.1, and into the Start Menu search box in Windows 7, and press Enter. The MMC as shown in Figure 5-13 will appear.

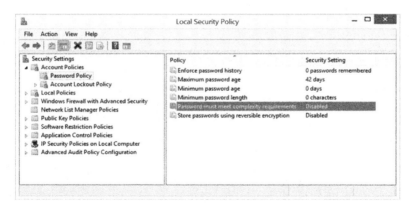

Figure 5-13. *Using Local Security Policy Editor to modify the password policy*

These complexity requirements can help ensure users have strong passwords that are significantly more difficult to crack, even by automated means. Where users need to regularly change their passwords, it can be helpful to suggest that they use passphrases to create long passwords that are easier to remember.

Summary

Maintaining effective and robust security on PCs is the best way to secure the Registry from attack by malware, hackers, or users who would do it harm. Security these days is multilayered, too, as we've detailed in this chapter.

Aside from all the seriousness, however, if you *did* want to hack your own Registry, what would you do with it? Well, in the final chapter we'll detail over 60 of our favorite cheats, hacks, tweaks, and Registry modifications.

CHAPTER 6

Hacks, Tweaks, and Common Changes

No operating system has ever been as configurable as Microsoft Windows. From its very earliest days you could change all manner of facets in its look, feel, and operation, and many of these have been made possible by the Registry.

You'll probably have your very own favorite Registry hacks and tweaks, which could do anything from modifying the look of the Windows User Interface (UI); to changing the operation of a feature, piece of software, or hardware device; or might even be a hack that modifies the underlying operation of Windows itself.

This chapter, then, is a grand compendium of our favorite hacks, tweaks, and changes, grouped with others that people have found useful or interesting over the years.

■ **Note**   Not all of these hacks will be relevant to all Windows editions. Where this is the case we will highlight this in the text by adding the version numbers at the start of the description.

It's worth noting that for all of these changes, you will either need to sign out and back in again if the change has been made to HKCU, or restart the PC if the Registry is change is made elsewhere. Also there are many tweaks here for File Explorer, which is called "Windows Explorer" in Windows Vista and Windows 7.

One word of warning: Before you implement any of the Registry tweaks here, or indeed any Registry tweak at all, make sure you export a backup copy of the Registry, or even just the affected key(s), so that you can restore these if the change you make causes a problem.

User Interface Tweaks

The most common hacks and tweaks in Windows will always involve the UI, and people have found a lot of them over the years. Here are some of the most popular, with our personal favorites.

Add Never Combine / Hide Labels to the Taskbar

(7, 8) The Windows Taskbar is great in how it handles icons and permits pinning of apps. However, it's missing a view that permits open apps to appear as separate icons without their descriptive text. You can add this, however, by changing the behavior of the Never Combine Hide Labels option; see Figures 6-1 and 6-2.

Figure 6-1. *The default Taskbar view in Windows*

Figure 6-2. *The modified Taskbar view for the same open apps*

To do this, navigate to [HKCU]\Control Panel\Desktop\WindowMetrics and create a string value called "MinWidth" with the value "54". You will need to sign out and back in again for this change to appear. If you are using desktop scaling on your PC change the value appropriately (e.g., for 150% scaling use 72, and for 125% scaling use the value 63).

Change Taskbar Program Preview Icons

(7, 8) When you hover your mouse over an icon for a running app on the Taskbar, the thumbnail image that appears can be resized to any pixel size you specify at the key [HKCU]\Software\Microsoft\Windows\CurrentVersion\Explorer\Taskband by adding a DWORD value named "MinThumbSizePx" and the value of the thumbnail size you want in pixels (e.g. 200 for large thumbnails or 400 for very large ones).

Change Taskbar Icons to Reopen Last Active Window

(7, 8) When you click a Taskbar icon and more than one instance of a program is running, you will be presented with thumbnails of all the running instances. You can change this behavior so that clicking the icon automatically displays the last running instance on the desktop (you can use Alt+Tab to switch to the others).

Navigate to [HKCU] \Software\Microsoft\Windows\CurrentVersion\Explorer\ Advanced and create a new DWORD value called "LastActiveClick" with a value of "1".

Change Peek Operation Time

(7) You can change the time it takes for Aero peek to display when you hover over its icon in the far right of the Taskbar at [HKCU] \Software\Microsoft\Windows\ CurrentVersion\Explorer\Advanced by creating a new DWORD value called "DesktopLivePreviewHoverTime" with a value in milliseconds (e.g., "200"). You can set it to activate instantly with the value "0".

Speed Up Appearance of Taskbar Thumbnail Icons

(7, 8) You can speed up the appearance of Taskbar app previews when you hover your mouse cursor over a running app, by going to [HKCU]\ Software\Microsoft\ Windows\CurrentVersion\Explorer\Advanced and creating a new DWORD value called "ExtendedUIHoverTime" that has the value of "1".

You can also slow down the appearance of the thumbnail previews by changing this value to a larger number, such as 500 or 1000. The number represents the time in milliseconds.

Show Classic "All Programs" in Start Menu

(Vista, 7) You can force the display of the XP-style All Programs menu at both [HKCU] \Software\Microsoft\Windows\CurrentVersion\Explorer\Shell Folders and [HKCU] HKEY_CURRENT_USER\Software\Microsoft\Windows\CurrentVersion\Explorer\User Shell Folders. Change the value of "Favorites" for both keys to "C:\ProgramData\ Microsoft\Windows\Start Menu\Programs".

Once you have made the change, right-click the Start button and click Properties from the context menu that appears. Under the Start Menu tab in the next dialog, click Advanced, and then in the list of options that appears, make sure Favorites menu is checked. You will need to restart your system for the change to take effect.

Pin Folders to the Start Menu

(Vista, 7) You can pin a folder to the Start Menu by going to the key [HKCR]\Folder\ shellex\ContextMenuHandlers and adding a new key called {a2a9545d-a0c2-42b4-9708-a0b2badd77c8}.

This will add a Pin to Start Menu option to the context menu for folders when you right-click them in Windows Explorer.

Disable Desktop Shake

(7, 8) Desktop shake, whereby you shake a window to minimize all others, can be annoying, especially for those with motor problems. It can be disabled in the Accessibility Options, but this can be difficult to find. Fortunately you can also disable it in the Registry at [HKCU]\ Software\Policies\Microsoft\Windows by adding a new subkey called Explorer in which you add a DWORD value called "NoWindowMinimizingShortcuts" with the value "1". The changes will take effect when you sign out and back in again.

Remove "Shortcut" Text from Shortcuts

(Vista, 7, 8) When you create a shortcut to a file or folder the text - Shortcut is automatically appended to its name. You can change this behavior at [HKCU] \Software\ Microsoft\Windows\CurrentVersion\Explorer where you will find a REG_BINARY value of "1e 00 00 00". Change this to "00 00 00 00" to implement the tweak.

Get Rid of Shortcut Arrow Icons

(Vista, 7, 8) Arrows on the icons of shortcuts are seen by many people as annoying, but you can remove them.

Navigate to [HKLM] \SOFTWARE\Microsoft\Windows\CurrentVersion\Explorer\ Shell Icons. If this key doesn't exist, you can create it. Create a string value called "29". The value for this should be C:\Windows\System32\shell32.dll,50. You will need to restart your PC to reset the icon cache before this will work.

Show Drive Letter Before Volume Name in File Explorer

(Vista, 7, 8) If you want to change the way File Explorer displays drive letters, so that they appear before the drive name rather than after it, navigate to [HKLM]\SOFTWARE\ Microsoft\Windows\CurrentVersion\Explorer and create a new DWORD called "ShowDriveLettersFirst" with the value "4".

Hide Drives in File Explorer

(Vista, 7, 8) You can hide any hard disk drive in File Explorer by navigating in the Registry to [HKCU] \Software\Microsoft\Windows\CurrentVersion\Policies\Explorer and adding a DWORD value called "NoDrives". This DWORD value will have a 32-bit number as its data that represents all the drives you wish to hide. The number you assign to the DWORD is the total of the drives you wish to hide; for example, hiding drives C and E will mean giving a value of 20 (4+16) as calculated using Table 6-1.

Table 6-1. *Hiding Drive letters in File Explorer*

Drive Letter	Number
A	1
B	2
C	4
D	8
E	16
F	32
G	64
H	128
I	256
J	512
K	1024
L	2048
M	4096
N	8192
O	16384
P	32768
Q	65536
R	131072
S	262144
T	524288
U	1048576
V	2097152
W	4194304
X	8388608
Y	16777216
Z	33554432
ALL	67108863

Show Recycle Bin in Computer View of File Explorer

(Vista, 7, 8) You can add the Recycle Bin to the Computer view in File Explorer by navigating to [HKLM] \SOFTWARE\Microsoft\Windows\CurrentVersion\Explorer\ MyComputer\NameSpace and creating a new key called {645FF040-5081-101B-9F08-00AA002F954E}.

Remove the "Use the Web Service to Find the Correct Program" Dialog

(Vista, 7) When Windows doesn't have a program or application associated with a specific file, it will ask if you want to search for one (Figure 6-3) or by a Windows Store pop-up in Windows 8 and 10.

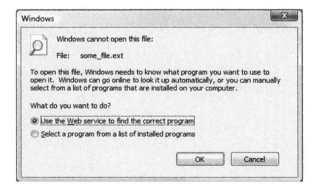

Figure 6-3. *The Use the Web service to find the correct program dialog*

You can prevent this message from appearing by navigating to [HKLM]\SOFTWARE\ Microsoft\Windows\CurrentVersion\Policies\Explorer and creating a new DWORD value called "NoInternetOpenWith" that has the value "1".

The result of making this change is that you will then automatically be presented with a list of installed programs and applications on your PC, and you can choose which one of these you wish to use to open the file.

Add Copy to.../Move to... to the File Explorer Context Menu

(Vista, 7, 8) You can add Copy to... and Move to... options to the context menu in File Explorer at the key [HKCR]\AllFilesystemObjects\shellex\ContextMenuHandlers and by adding new keys called "CopyToFolder" with the value {C2FBB630-2971-11D1-A18C-00C04FD75D13} and "MoveToFolder" with the value {C2FBB631-2971-11D1-A18C-00C04FD75D13}.

Add Open with Notepad to File Explorer Context Menu

(Vista, 7, 8) You can add an "Open with Notepad" option to the Context Menu when right-clicking files at [HKCR]*\Shell by creating a subkey called "Open with Notepad" that has a subkey called "command" with the data for the Default string value "notepad.exe %1".

Add Defragment to the File Explorer Context Menu

(Vista, 7, 8) Add a defragment option to the File Explorer context menu when right-clicking disks at [HKCR]\Drive\shell and by creating a new subkey called "runas". Double-click this to open it and change its Default string value to "Defragment", and create a subkey under that called "command" with the following data for its Default string value: "defrag %1 -v".

Add Command Prompt to the File Explorer Context Menu

(Vista, 7, 8) To add an Open Command Prompt option to context menus when you right-click a folder in File Explorer, navigate to [HKLM]\Software\Classes\Folder\Shell and create a new subkey called "CommandPrompt". Double-click this to open it and change the data for its Default string value to "Open Command Prompt here...".

Next, create a subkey under this called "command" with the following data for its Default string value: "cmd.exe /k pushd %L".

Disable the Send to... Menu in File Explorer

(Vista, 7, 8) You can disable the Send to... option in File Explorer context menus by navigating to [HKCR] \AllFilesystemObjects\shellex\ContextMenuHandlers\Send To. Double-click the Default value for this key and delete its contents. You can later restore it by changing its contents back to {7BA4C740-9E81-11CF-99D3-00AA004AE837}.

Hide Unwanted Apps from the File Explorer Context Menus

(Vista, 7, 8) Installed programs can push themselves in your Context Menus and clutter them. You can remove these additional items at the following Registry locations; alas, they're not all stored in one place together:

[HKCR]*\shell
[HKCR]*\shellex\ContextMenuHandlers
[HKCR]\AllFileSystemObjects\ShellEx

Under these locations you will see subkeys for the third-party software that has plugged itself into your context menus. There are several ways to handle them. You can delete the keys to remove them completely. To force them to show only on a Shift+right click, add a string value to each called "Extended", or to leave them in the Registry but disable them, add a string value called "LegacyDisable".

Remove Troubleshoot Compatibility from File Explorer Context Menu

(Vista, 7, 8) You may not want the Troubleshoot Compatibility option to display in the context menu for apps and can disable it at both [HKCR] \exefile\ shellex\ContextMenuHandlers\Compatibility and [HKCR] lnkfile\shellex\ ContextMenuHandlers\Compatibility by adding a dash "-" to the beginning of the key value for each.

Remove Programs from Open with... Context Menu

(Vista, 7, 8) If you want to remove programs from the Open with... menu that appears when you right-click a file, navigate to [HKCU]\Software\Microsoft\Windows\ CurrentVersion\Explorer\FileExts where you will see subkeys for all known file extension types.

In this list of subkeys, look for "OpenWithList" and you can delete values in this list for the programs you wish to remove from the context menu.

Add Copy to Clipboard Option to File Explorer Context Menu

(Vista, 7, 8) Sometimes you want to copy a file to the computer's Clipboard, but if you press Ctrl+C it will copy the whole file. Adding a Copy to Clipboard option in your File Explorer context menu will instead copy what's *inside* that file.

To add a Copy to Clipboard option, navigate to [HKCR]\txtfile\shell where you should create a subkey called "CopyToClip" with Copy to Clipboard for its Default string value.

Under the CopyToClip subkey, create an additional subkey called "command" with the following data for its Default string value: "cmd /c clip < "%1"".

Remove Items from IE Context Menu

(Vista, 7, 8) It's not just File Explorer that can have messy and slow-to-open context menus; Internet Explorer can, too. You can tidy it by navigating to [HKCU] \Software\ Microsoft\Internet Explorer\MenuExt, where you will find subkeys for browser plug-ins that have added themselves to the menu. You can delete these subkeys to remove the associated menu option.

App Tweaks

Sometimes specific apps will come with their own Registry tweaks. Two useful and common ones are the options to remove the Context menu entries for AMD and Nvidia display cards.

Remove AMD Catalyst Control Center from Desktop Context Menu

(Vista, 7, 8) To remove the AMD Catalyst Control Center option, navigate to [HKCR] \Directory\Background\shellex\ContextMenuHandlers\ACE and double-click the Default value. Then add a dash "-" to the beginning of the value to disable the item.

Remove NVIDIA Control Panel from Desktop Context Menu

(Vista, 7, 8) To remove the Nvidia Control Panel item from context menus, navigate to [HKCR]\Directory\Background\shellex\ContextMenuHandlers\, where you can delete the key "NvCplDesktopContext".

Administrative Tweaks

It's common knowledge that tasks that can be accomplished in Group Policy, can also be achieved through the use of Registry tweaks. This isn't the limit of the administrative tweaks that can be performed in Registry however, and here are our favorites.

Prevent Windows Update from Restarting the PC Automatically

(Vista, 7, 8) Windows Update can be annoying. Even in Windows 8 and 10 where it's less prone to automatically restart your PC when you don't want it to. You can prevent Windows Update from being able to restart a PC completely, however, at [HKLM]\SOFTWARE\Policies\Microsoft\Windows\WindowsUpdate\AU. If this key doesn't exist, you can create it. Next, create a DWORD value called "NoAutoRebootWithLoggedOnUsers" and give it the value "1" as its data.

Stop Windows Update from Hijacking Your Shut Down/Restart Options

(Vista, 7, 8) When Windows Update has updates to install, it will alert you by modifying the Shut Down and Restart options in the Start Menu or at the Start screen with an icon or some text.

This can sometimes change the default button, which often is set to Sleep. But you can disable Windows's ability to change this button by navigating to [HKCU] \Software\ Policies\Microsoft\Windows\WindowsUpdate\AU and adding a DWORD value called "NoAUAsDefaultShutdownOption" with "1" as its data.

Disable the Shut Down Command

(Vista, 7, 8) You can disable the Shut Down command in the Start Menu and Start screen at the key [HKCU]\Software\Microsoft\Windows\CurrentVersion\Policies\Explorer by creating a DWORD value called "NoClose" with "1" as its data.

Hide Unwanted Items from the Control Panel

(Vista, 7, 8) Many items can be hidden from the Control Panel using a Registry hack at the key [HKLM]\SOFTWARE\Microsoft\Windows\CurrentVersion\Control Panel\don't load. You can create it if it doesn't exist. You can add a new string value for each one you wish to hide (see Table 6-2).

Table 6-2. *Control Panel Applet Names*

Control Panel Applet	Name of String Key
Accessibility Options	access.cpl
Add New Hardware Wizard	hdwiz.cpl
Display Properties	desk.cpl
Game Controllers	joy.cpl
Internet Options	inetcpl.cpl
Mouse Properties	main.cpl
Network Connections	ncpa.cpl
ODBC Data Sources	odbccp32.cpl
Phone and Modem Options	telephon.cpl
Power Options	powercfg.cpl
Programs and Features	appwiz.cpl
Region	intl.cpl
Sound	mmsys.cpl
Speech	sapi.cpl
System	sysdm.cpl
Time and Date	timedate.cpl
User Accounts	nusrmgr.cpl

Add RegEdit to the Control Panel

(Vista, 7, 8) A Windows Registry book wouldn't be complete without a Registry tweak, and here's one that allows you to add a direct link to the Registry Editor to the Control Panel.

Open a blank Notepad file and write the following text into it.

```
Windows Registry Editor Version 5.00
[HKEY_CLASSES_ROOT\CLSID\{77708248-f839-436b-8919-527c410f48b9}]
@="Registry Editor"
"InfoTip"="Starts the Registry Editor"
"System.ControlPanel.Category"="5"
[HKEY_CLASSES_ROOT\CLSID\{77708248-f839-436b-8919-527c410f48b9}\DefaultIcon]
@="%SYSTEMROOT%\\regedit.exe"
[HKEY_CLASSES_ROOT\CLSID\{77708248-f839-436b-8919-527c410f48b9}\Shell]
[HKEY_CLASSES_ROOT\CLSID\{77708248-f839-436b-8919-527c410f48b9}\Shell\Open]
[HKEY_CLASSES_ROOT\CLSID\{77708248-f839-436b-8919-527c410f48b9}\Shell\Open\
Command]
@=hex(2):25,00,53,00,79,00,73,00,74,00,65,00,6d,00,52,00,6f,00,6f,00,74,00,
25,\00,5c,00,72,00,65,00,67,00,65,00,64,00,69,00,74,00,2e,00,65,00,78,00,
65,00,\00,00
[HKEY_LOCAL_MACHINE\SOFTWARE\Microsoft\Windows\CurrentVersion\Explorer\
ControlPanel\NameSpace\{77708248-f839-436b-8919-527c410f48b9}]
@="Add Registry Editor to Control Panel"
```

Now save this file as a `.reg` file; by default Notepad will want to save it as a `.txt` file, so in the Save dialog choose All file types instead.

You can also remove the Registry Editor from the control panel by creating a `.reg` file with the following contents.

```
Windows Registry Editor Version 5.00
[-HKEY_CLASSES_ROOT\CLSID\{77708248-f839-436b-8919-527c410f48b9}]
[-HKEY_LOCAL_MACHINE\SOFTWARE\Microsoft\Windows\CurrentVersion\Explorer\
ControlPanel\NameSpace\{77708248-f839-436b-8919-527c410f48b9}]
```

Add Control Panel to Computer Display in File Explorer

(Vista, 7, 8) You can add a link to the Control Panel to the Computer view in File Explorer by navigating to [HKLM] \SOFTWARE\Microsoft\Windows\CurrentVersion\Explorer\ MyComputer\NameSpace where you should create a new subkey called either {26EE0668-A00A-44D7-9371-BEB064C98683} if you want the Category view for the Control Panel, or {21EC2020-3AEA-1069-A2DD-08002B30309D} if you instead want the Icon view.

Add Control Panel to the Desktop Context Menu

(Vista, 7, 8) You can also add a link to Control Panel in the desktop context menu by navigating to [HKCR]\Directory\Background\shell where you'll want to create a new subkey called Control Panel. In this subkey create an extra subkey called "command" and when you see its default value, change this to "rundll32.exe shell32.dll,Control_RunDLL".

Add Take Ownership to File Explorer Context Menu

(Vista, 7, 8) File and folder ownership in Windows can often be a problem, and taking ownership of those files and folders so you can access or work on them can be fiddly. You can add a quick link to taking ownership of files though by copying the following text into a blank notepad file, and saving that file with a .reg extension.

```
[HKEY_CLASSES_ROOT\*\shell\runas]
@="Take Ownership"
"NoWorkingDirectory"=""
[HKEY_CLASSES_ROOT\*\shell\runas\command]
@="cmd.exe /c takeown /f \"%1\" && icacls \"%1\" /grant administrators:F"
"IsolatedCommand"="cmd.exe /c takeown /f \"%1\" && icacls \"%1\" /grant
administrators:F"
[HKEY_CLASSES_ROOT\Directory\shell\runas]
@="Take Ownership"
"NoWorkingDirectory"=""
[HKEY_CLASSES_ROOT\Directory\shell\runas\command]
@="cmd.exe /c takeown /f \"%1\" /r /d y && icacls \"%1\" /grant
administrators:F /t"
"IsolatedCommand"="cmd.exe /c takeown /f \"%1\" /r /d y && icacls \"%1\"
/grant administrators:F /t"
```

Disable all Taskbar Balloon Notifications

(Vista, 7, 8) Windows 10 might include a handy notification center, but for people using Vista, Windows 7 or Windows 8, Taskbar popup alerts can still be annoying.

You can disable them by navigating to [HKCU] \Software\Microsoft\ Windows\CurrentVersion\Explorer\Advanced and creating a new DWORD called "EnableBalloonTips" with "0" as its data.

Change the Registered Owner Name for Your Windows Installation

(Vista, 7, 8) Sometimes you might find you want to change the name of the registered owner of a copy of Windows. You can do this at [HKLM] \SOFTWARE\Microsoft\ Windows NT\CurrentVersion by changing the text for the "RegisteredOwner" and "RegisteredOrganization" values. You can check the current owner by typing winver.exe at the command prompt or in the Start Menu search box.

Disable the Mobility Center

(Vista, 7, 8) Battery life on laptops and tablets is crucial, and you might have carefully crafted a battery saving plan that you don't want your users to change. You can disable access to the Windows Mobility Center at [HKCU] \Software\Microsoft\Windows\ CurrentVersion\Policies\MobilityCenter by creating a new DWORD value called "NoMobilityCenter" with "1" as its data.

Force Disk Cleanup to Delete All Temporary Files

(Vista, 7, 8) Did you know that when you use the Disk Cleanup wizard in Windows it only deletes temporary files that are more than seven days old? Well, you can change this behavior at [HKLM]\SOFTWARE\Microsoft\Windows\ CurrentVersion\Explorer\ VolumeCaches\Temporary Files by changing the "LastAccess" value from the default 7 to another number, such as 1 or 0.

Add Encrypt/Decrypt Options to File Explorer Context Menu

(Vista, 7, 8) If you use Microsoft's Encrypted File System (EFS) to encrypt files on your PC, you can add Encrypt and Decrypt options to the context menu when you right-click a file in File Explorer. To do this, navigate to [HKCU] \Software\Microsoft\ Windows\CurrentVersion\Explorer\Advanced and create a new DWORD value called "EncryptionContextMenu" that has "1" as its data.

Force Verbose Message During Startup and Shutdown

(Vista, 7, 8) When Windows starts and shuts down you don't get any information these days about what it's actually doing, such as shutting down services or the user profile. You can force Windows to give you more verbose messages instead at [HKLM]\SOFTWARE\ Microsoft\Windows\CurrentVersion\Policies\System by creating a DWORD value called "VerboseStatus" that has "1" as its data.

Enable/Disable Task Manager link from Taskbar Context Menu

(Vista, 7, 8) Sometimes you might want to deny users access to the Task Manager. You can disable the Task Manager link that appears in the context menu on a right-click of the Taskbar. Navigate to [HKCU]\Software\Microsoft\Windows\CurrentVersion\Policies\ System and change the DWORD called "DisableTaskMgr" to "1" to disable the link or "0" to enable it.

Display a Message During Windows Startup

(Vista, 7, 8) Probably of most use to companies and enterprises, you can force Windows to display a text message at boot time, such as company information by navigating to [HKLM]\Software\Microsoft\Windows\Current Version\Policies\System and changing the text values of "legalnoticecaption" and "legalnoticetext".

Disable the Last Access File Timestamp

(Vista, 7) The last accessed file timestamp can be a pain, especially if you use a cloud service such as Microsoft's OneDrive to keep backup copies of files that you access regularly, such as music. Every time a file is opened (or a music track played) it registers as a file change, and this can force cloud backup software to reload the file all over again.

To disable the last accessed file change, navigate to [HKLM]\SYSTEM\CurrentControlSet\Control\Filesystem and change the data of NtfsDisableLastAccessUpdate from 0 to 1.

Disable Low Disk Space Warning

(Vista, 7, 8) Sometimes, especially on small Windows tablets with small amounts of internal storage, you will get regular and annoying pop-up alerts warning you of "low disk space." You can disable these at [HKCU]\Software\Microsoft\Windows\CurrentVersion by adding a DWORD value called "NoLowDiskSpaceChecks" and specifying "1" as its data.

Disable the Windows Security Center/Action Center

(Vista, 7, 8) I genuinely cannot think of when you might want to do this except for some enterprise environments where you already have strict controls on security on your PCs and laptops. However, the Windows Security Center can be disabled at [HKLM]\SYSTEM\CurrentControlSet\Services\wscsvc by changing the data of the "Start" value from "2" to "4".

Disable Windows Malicious Software Removal Tool Anonymous Reporting

(Vista, 7, 8) When you download and run the Windows Malicious Software Removal Tool, it silently reports back to Microsoft on what it's done. If you don't want it to do this, navigate to [HKLM]\SOFTWARE\Policies\Microsoft\MRT and create a DWORD value called "DontReportInfectionInformation" that has "1" as its data.

Disable IPv6

(Vista, 7, 8) The world needs IPv6, with so many laptops, tablets, fridges, cars, and microwaves now connected to the Internet. In some environments, however, such as where legacy hardware or software encounters problems with IPv6 in Windows, you can disable it at [HKLM]\SYSTEM\CurrentControlSet\Services\Tcpip6\Parameters\ by creating a DWORD value called "DisabledComponents" that has "ffffff" as its value.

Force Windows Drives to Use AHCI

(Vista, 7, 8) Similarly you might find that for compatibility reasons you need your drives to be using the Advanced Host Controller Interface (AHCI). To force this, navigate to [HKLM]\SYSTEM\CurrentControlSet\services\msahci and create a DWORD called "Start" with the value "0".

Disable "Do You Want to Run This File" Dialog

(Vista, 7, 8) When you download a file from the Internet you will be asked if you really want to run the file when you open it. Well, given that you *did* open it, it's probably quite likely that you did, so you can disable this message by copying this text into a blank Notepad file and saving it with a .reg file extension.

```
[HKEY_CURRENT_USER\Software\Microsoft\Internet Explorer\Download]
"CheckExeSignatures"="no"
"RunInvalidSignatures"=dword:00000001
[HKEY_CURRENT_USER\Software\Microsoft\Windows\CurrentVersion\Policies\
Attachments]
"SaveZoneInformation"=dword:00000001
[HKEY_CURRENT_USER\Software\Microsoft\Windows\CurrentVersion\Policies\
Associations]
"LowRiskFileTypes"=".zip;.rar;.nfo;.txt;.exe;.bat;.com;.cmd;.reg;.msi;.htm;.
html;.gif;.bmp;.jpg;.avi;.mpg;.mpeg;.mov;.mp3;.m3u;.wav;"
```

Force-Writing to "Write Protected" USB Flash Drives

(Vista, 7, 8) Sometimes you might find that you can't write to a USB flash drive because writing to these drives is forbidden in Group Policy. Instead you can tell Windows to always ignore this protection by navigating to [HKLM]\SYSTEM\CurrentControlSet\Control\ StorageDevicePolicies and changing the value of the key "WriteProtect" to "0".

You will also need to navigate to [HKLM]\SYSTEM\ControlSet00?\Control\ StorageDevicePolicies where 00? represents the different numbered subkeys. You will need to change all of the values "WriteProtect" to "0". If this key doesn't exist you can create it.

Activate "God Mode" in Windows

(Vista, 7, 8) God Mode isn't actually a Registry tweak, but it's so popular that we couldn't really leave it out. This creates a folder containing every individual Control Panel and Administrative item that's available in Windows. You can create it by putting a new folder on the desktop called "God Mode .{ED7BA470-8E54-465E-825C-99712043E01C}". Once the new folder has been created you can modify the folder name to anything you chose.

Performance Tweaks

(Vista, 7, 8) Some tweaks are designed to boost the performance of Windows and your PC. Here is a selection of some of the best and some of our favorites.

Increase the Maximum Allowed HTTP File Transfers

(Vista, 7, 8) By default, Windows restricts the number of simultaneous HTTP file transfers over the Internet to just two. Most web browsers change this limit for themselves, but if you're transferring files over HTTP from within a program such as File Explorer you'll hit the two-file transfer limit. You can change this by copying the following text into a blank Notepad file and then saving that file with a .reg extension.

```
Windows Registry Editor Version 5.00
[HKEY_CURRENT_USER\Software\Microsoft\Windows\CurrentVersion\Internet
Settings]
"MaxConnectionsPer1_0Server"=dword:00000012
"MaxConnectionsPerServer"=dword:00000012
```

Maximize Your Internet Bandwidth

(Vista, 7, 8) Did you know that Windows reserves up to 20% of your Internet bandwidth for itself? Well you can disable this and maximize the available Internet bandwidth at [HKLM]\SOFTWARE\Policies\Microsoft\Windows\Psched by creating a DWORD value called "NonBestEffortLimit" that has "0" as its data.

Force Windows to Auto-End Tasks on Shutdown

(Vista, 7, 8) You can force Windows to shut down more quickly by adding this Registry key. Note however that if you have unsaved files and documents still open, this can force the program to quit before the file is saved. In [HKCU]\Control Panel\Desktop add a new DWORD value called "AutoEndTasks" and set its data as "1".

Reduce the WaitToKill Time for Closing Apps

(Vista, 7, 8) Again, when shutting down your PC it might take some time for apps to close. You can reduce this time and shut down the PC faster by adding the DWORD value "WaitToKillAppTimeout" to [HKCU]\Control Panel\Desktop and giving it a data of "2000". This is the time is in milliseconds and, as with the last tweak, this could result in unsaved files not being saved before the PC shuts down.

Reduce Time to Kill a Hung App or Process

(Vista, 7, 8) When an app is hung and unresponsive, Windows can wait some time to shut it down. You can reduce this time by adding the DWORD value "HungAppTimeout" to [HKCU]\Control Panel\Desktop and giving it the data "1000", which is in milliseconds.

Reduce the Time Taken to Stop a Windows Service

(Vista, 7, 8) Windows Services can be shut down more quickly too by adding the DWORD value "WaitToKillServiceTimeout" to [HKLM]\SYSTEM\CurrentControlSet\Control with the millisecond data "2000".

Fun Tweaks

Lastly, we thought we'd include a few tweaks that exist purely for fun. We have no idea why you'd want to do these other than to play a practical joke on somebody, so if you do please be responsible and set things back afterward.

Enable More Fonts in Command Prompt

(Vista, 7, 8) This first tweak is likely the most useful as it allows you to expand the number of fonts you can use in a Command Prompt window. This can have many uses including making text in the window easier to read. Navigate to [HKLM]\SOFTWARE\Microsoft\ WindowsNT\CurrentVersion\Console\TrueTypeFont and you will see a list of fonts. Create a new string value named "00" and change its data to the name of the font you wish to use, for example "Consolas". This will only work with fixed-width fonts, so not all fonts are compatible.

Disable the Caps Lock Key

(Vista, 7, 8) If you hate your Caps Lock key and keep hitting it by accident, which we all do now and again, you can disable it at [HKLM]\SYSTEM\CurrentControlSet\Control\ Keyboard Layout by changing the data of "Scancode Map" to "000000000 00000000 02000000 00003A00 00000000".

Force Windows XP-Style Classic Login Dialog

(Vista, 7) Some people prefer the classic Windows XP-style logon screen in Windows, and you can bring it back by adding the DWORD value "dontdisplaylastusername" with the data "1" to [HKLM]\SOFTWARE\Microsoft\Windows\CurrentVersion\Policies\System.

Control System Tray Icons Using the Registry

(Vista, 7, 8) You can hide any of the four system tray icons at [HKCU]\Software\Microsoft\Windows\CurrentVersion\Policies\ by creating keys called "HideSCAVolume", "HideSCAPower", "HideSCANetwork", and "HideSCAHealth", giving each "0" as the data for its Default value.

Force a Blue Screen of Death in Three Keystrokes

(Vista, 7, 8) Lastly, the pièce de résistance for Windows users, forcing a blue screen of death in three keystrokes. This is actually more useful than it sounds, as forcing a BSOD will create a memory dump file that can be used by System Administrators for testing purposes.

Navigate to [HKLM]\SYSTEM\CurrentControlSet\Services\kbdhid\Parameters and create a DWORD value called "CrashOnCtrlScroll" that has a data of "1". After a reboot, when you hold down Right Ctrl and press Scroll Lock twice, a BSOD will be triggered.

Summary

These are just a few of the thousands of Registry hacks and tweaks that are available for Windows users and system administrators. If you have a favorite you'd like to see included in the next edition of this book, then by all means contact us and let us know what it is.

Index

Get the eBook for only $10!

Now you can take the weightless companion with you anywhere, anytime. Your purchase of this book entitles you to 3 electronic versions for only $10.

This Apress title will prove so indispensible that you'll want to carry it with you everywhere, which is why we are offering the eBook in 3 formats for only $10 if you have already purchased the print book.

Convenient and fully searchable, the PDF version enables you to easily find and copy code—or perform examples by quickly toggling between instructions and   applications. The MOBI format is ideal for your Kindle, while the ePUB can be utilized on a variety of mobile devices.

Go to www.apress.com/promo/tendollars to purchase your companion eBook.

CPSIA information can be obtained at www.ICGtesting.com
Printed in the USA
LVOW04s1612030515

437065LV00003B/11/P

33164100038251

9 781484 209936